CW00391281

THE KITCHEN THERAPIST

For the Love of Chicken

For my children!

THE KITCHEN THERAPIST

For the Love of Chicken

Jo Richardson

NEW HOLLAND

ACKNOWLEDGEMENT

A second book in two years! I have to thank New Holland for believing in me and offering me this title (as I do really love the stuff). This book has allowed me to showcase my chicken favourites and share.

Linda Williams, you have steered me through again. I love your insight, knowledge of your industry, trust and helpfulness to authors and I also have to mention your wonderful cheeky sense of humour.

Thanks to my dear family for eating and eating and eating as I tested and tweaked. Only towards the very end did my daughter declare 'not tonight Mama—I can't eat it anymore'!

Thanks also to my husband and girlfriends for listening to me talk about nothing but chicken! And special mention to Jan and Janine for their constant belief and encouragement. To my clients (old and new), especially Peter McInnes, who sat by patiently waiting for me to have a 'spare moment' to complete a deadline or promised recipe.

Sally Lukey, you're an angel. I thank you for it all, especially your eagle eye for detail, wonderful enthusiasm and dedication. I do love the giggles we have too. And the constant trail of emails titled 'Bok Bok Bok' made me smile.

To dear Kev, a remarkable cook with a knowledge and passion I so admire. You also have the best cook book reference library I know and your generous open-door policy is so appreciated, thank you for your constant support.

The photography team, your beautiful work is seen here in every image and recipe—thank you Joe, Georgie and Jo (Forrest). Lilydale CHicken, without your superb free-range chicken, my recipes couldn't taste as divine! Thank you team from the bottom of my heart.

From my kitchen to yours, I hope you all love every mouthful.

TABLE OF CONTENTS

INTRODUCTION

Years ago chicken was 'special' occasion food. As a small child, I remember chicken as a treat. In today's kitchen that has changed, chicken is now more widely eaten than many other meats—white or red. Not only sold in specialty poultry stores but each and every supermarket and just about every local butcher too.

Goodness, there are so many recipes for chicken, where should I start? I thought about the classics I love, the recipes we all want, admire or have heard of. From soups to salads, stir-fries to roasts, char-grilling to deep frying—the list of chicken possibilities is endless.

I must make mention of the fact right here and now that you won't find a recipe for chicken parmigiana in this book. I believe that this is the quintessential pub meal. Pop down to your local, grab a beer and enjoy one there when you fancy it.

In this book, I have followed the style from my first *Mastering the Basics*. I have listed the equipment you will need for each recipe and included tips throughout. I have also included a few 'Fixing What Went Wrong' hints to help you fix any cooking troubles you may have had. If we can reduce the wrongs, all our cooking and recipes will be better and cheaper. Food is expensive and it's quite silly to cook something badly, or with ordinary results. So let's make more of the good and less of the not so good.

My last meal would be chicken—a wonderful roast chicken, with golden crispy skin and soft succulent flesh is the meal for me, every time.

Before I go, I need to share with you that one of my nicknames (given to me by a cheeky food photographer) is actually 'chicken hawk'. So it seems this book was meant to be!

Jo

Good quality chicken

Free-range is absolutely essential.

A reliable food processor

And for me it's KitchenAid®.

Heavy based cookware

Frying pan, braising pan, char grill.

Salt flakes

I especially love pink salt flakes, but I use rock salt and ground salt also.

Fresh lemons and limes

For the zing and flavour balance.

A range of oils

From coconut to peanut and extra virgin olive oil with everything in between!

Of course there is so much more, but I said six!

THE SIX THINGS I CAN'T LIVE WITHOUT

CHICKEN CHOICES

When buying chicken, we make choices about the quality of the meat. It pays to be fussy.

The flavour and texture of a happy, free-range bird simply can't be compared to a farmed bird. Apart from many ethical factors, the flavour and texture of an organic or free-range chicken speaks volumes.

We can make a choice and scream it out loudly too! The more we all speak and take a stand the less of these awful bird farms will exist. This is the case for eggs too.

Quality

Buy the best you can afford. A must. There is no mistaking good quality. Good chicken has a look and 'feel' to it. The skin is firm, the flesh is pink and somehow bright looking. Smell—absolutely none! Corn-fed chicken will of course have a yellow (not pink) tinge to the flesh.

Shop Ethically

I personally believe the bird deserves to wander around, flap its wings, scratch the ground and eat freely. This freedom is not only so important for the wellbeing of the bird, it also affects the flavour and texture and that's as equally important to me.

Read, explore, talk to your fresh food merchant, chat with your favourite chef, ask at your local café, find out what chicken they are buying?

Read the labels on the packaging. If they are good, you'll see and you'll taste it.

Taste

The taste of what you are eating is so important. I would rather eat a little less of something good, than lots of something that is tasteless and bland. So if your budget is tight, serve a little less of the chicken and bulk up the meal with potatoes, rice and vegetables. One or two glorious forkfuls of superb mouth-watering, succulent chicken is often all you need. You can make better choices at ready to go 'charcoal chicken' stores too. The cooked barbecue ready to go at the supermarket even has choice.

You can cook chicken in just about any way you wish: pan fry, stir fry, shallow fry, deep-fry, braise, poach, simmer, char-grill, roast or barbecue. But different cuts of chicken work for different cooking methods. Each cut comes with a section of fat. It can be seen on the sides of the pieces (such as the thighs and the breast) or sometimes under the skin. It is up to you to trim or retain this fat if you wish, but remember the fat adds flavour and succulence. Remove it all and you must take care not to dry the flesh out. I prefer to cook with the extra fat but not eat it, so as to get as much flavour as I can.

THE WHOLE BIRD: The standard size used in this book is a size 16 (3½ lb/1.6 kg). Usually, a standard bird is size 14 (3 lb/1.4 kg to a 4 lb/1.8 kg). If using a smaller or larger bird, decrease or increase the cooking time to suit.

BREAST FILLET: Usually sold separately (large fillets are around 10 oz/280 g each)

How to use: braise, barbecue, pan-fry, char-grill.

THIGH FILLET: My favourite cut. Sold with the skin on or off. I find the thigh fillet has more flavour and texture than the breast fillet. In this book, I've used them extensively as they are flavoursome, affordable and meaty! The thigh simply doesn't dry out as quickly and can be cooked in all recipes and styles.

How to use: stir-fry, pan-fry, braise, barbecue, char-grill.

THIGH: Usually sold as they are, in a whole piece, with the bones (back and thigh bone) left in and skin on.

How to use: roast, braise, barbecue, char-grill, pan-fry, crumb and deep- or shallow-fry.

THIGH CUTLET: Usually sold with the backbone removed but the thigh bone left in and the skin on. Daintier looking than the whole thigh.

How to use: roast, braise, char-grill, barbecue.

MARYLAND: An economical cut. Very flavoursome and remains succulent due to the thigh meat. Normally sold with the thigh bone in and the leg (drumstick bone in), skin on.

How to use: roast, barbecue, braise.

DRUMSTICK: The base of the leg itself. Economical cut. Sold with the bone in and skin on.

How to use: braise, roast, barbecued, crumbed and deep-fried.

WINGS: Affordable cut, with little meat. Sold with three sections, often the 'end tip' is best trimmed off and discarded. Always sold with the skin on.

How to use: simmer, braise, barbecue, crumb and deep-fry.

CARCASS: The entire bone structure from the whole bird. All bone with little or no flesh left on the bones.

How to use: for chicken stock.

CHICKEN CUTS

PREPARATION RULES

Remove all the packaging from the chicken.

The chicken may be wrapped in plastic wrap for a whole bird or a plastic bag for fresh pieces from the butcher or poultry shop. Or you may have bought it on a tray, which stops the meat from sticking together. Whichever way it comes, you will want to remove any unwanted liquid or moisture from the chicken.

Don't leave the chicken in its original packing.

If you leave the chicken clumped in a plastic bag, or wrapped inside white paper, the cold air in the refrigerator can't circulate around the meat. This is a huge health hazard and can lead to the growth of bacteria that causes food poisoning.

Re-shape: When you remove the chicken from the packaging, pat it dry and re-shape it. It makes storing and working with the chicken so much nicer.

Line a plate or storage container with paper towel.

If any moisture escapes from the chicken it will be absorbed. You don't want the chicken sitting in any of its juices (particularly not blood). Lay the chicken on the paper towel, cover with plastic wrap or the lid to the container and refrigerate quickly. Don't place anything on top of the chicken (give it a little room)! The air must circulate around the plate or container to help keep it cool.

In the fridge: You may have a special section in the fridge for meats and chicken. Otherwise, I keep the chicken on a shelf that is clearly visible, so I don't forget about it.

Use within 2 days maximum and always store between 0–4°C.

Any look of moisture or any kind of smell what so ever—don't use, just throw it out. Chicken must be super fresh, plump, pink and feel fresh!

Freezing

Remove the chicken from the packaging, dry with a paper towel and lay flat. If the chicken is in a purpose-made tray, freeze the chicken in this tray. Expel as much air as possible. Wrap the chicken firmly in the plastic or specified freezer wrapping, with as little air trapped in as possible. You also want no liquid on the chicken, as this will form ice. Don't wrap in paper towel as this will stick to the chicken.

Once the chicken is wrapped up, label with the date and it helps to name the chicken cut too (frozen packages can all look the same in the freezer). You can freeze chicken for a maximum of 3 months.

Defrosting Rules

Remove from the freezer and separate individual pieces, if you only want one or two. After doing this, expel the extra air and secure the bag again, quickly putting the remainder of the chicken back into the freezer.

If possible, remove the wrapper or covering from the piece of chicken you wish to use, place the frozen chicken onto a plate in the refrigerator and leave it for a couple of hours. Remove the wrapping now, if you weren't able to before. In cooler weather, I will put the chicken on the plate and place in a clean kitchen sink. But if it's warm, the fridge is the safest option.

Do not let the chicken sit in clammy wet juices. The chicken needs to be wiped as soon as possible, placed onto dry paper towel on a clean plate and lightly covered until ready to use—just as if you were starting with

fresh chicken that has not been frozen. It will often take a day or overnight to defrost completely. Note: It is dangerous to put the chicken out on the bench or in the sun! Defrosting this way will encourage bacteria growth and the chicken will defrost unevenly.

Microwave defrosting: I'm not a fan of this, especially with chicken, so I do not recommend it. But if you do have to do it, remove all the wrappings, place on a plate and defrost on the lowest setting possible and as slow as possible. I find it does terrible things mostly so I like the fridge method!

Once defrosted, always use within 1–2 days. Never freeze chicken, defrost and freeze again—even if the chicken has been cooked. Freezing is a once-off thing.

Chicken and Bacteria

I don't want to scare you but it's a fact that all chicken is susceptible to the growth of very harmful bacteria. So treat the bird with your best good hygiene rules.

Shopping: Be prepared and take a freezer brick and an insulated bag (or purchase one at the store) with you when shopping for chicken or meat.

Once home, use clean washed hands to remove the chicken from the packaging and store correctly in the refrigerator (see above). Refrigerate at 0–4°C.

Utensils

A separate chopping board, plate and cook's knife should always be used for raw chicken. Once the chicken is prepared, always wash the utensils in hot soapy water. Never use the same utensils for raw and cooked foods.

A
BITE
TO
EAT

Originally created in Boston, USA, these 'punchy' wings are now a favourite everywhere!

Serves 4
Cooking style: Bake

Equipment: chopping board, cook's knife and/ or cleaver, large mixing bowl, medium saucepan, measuring spoons and cups, scales, 2 large baking dishes, tongs, slotted spoon, plastic wrap, baking paper

3 lb 5oz/1.5 kg free range chicken wings
3½ fl oz/100 ml vegetable oil (sunflower or light olive oil)
2 teaspoons cayenne pepper
1 tablespoon Worcestershire sauce
3 teaspoons salt flakes
2 teaspoons freshly ground black pepper

Hot Barbecue Sauce

2 tablespoons olive oil
1 large onion, very finely chopped
3 cloves garlic, finely chopped
1 teaspoon ground cumin
1 teaspoon cayenne pepper

1 tablespoon brown vinegar or apple cider vinegar
1 tablespoon Dijon mustard
1 tablespoon Worcestershire sauce
3 tablespoons brown sugar
4 fl oz/125 ml tomato puree
5 fl oz/150 ml water

Preheat the oven to 420°F/220°C (400°F/200°C fan-forced).

Using a large knife or cleaver, cut off the wing tip, just on the middle joint and discard.

Combine the oil, cayenne, Worcestershire sauce, salt and pepper in the large bowl and coat the chicken wings in the mixture so they are completely covered. (I do this with clean hands, to make sure the wings are coated well.)

Cover with plastic wrap and refrigerate for 2 hours (or longer, if time allows) to marinate.

Line 2 large baking dishes (base and sides) with

baking paper. Lightly drain the wings from any excess marinade using the slotted spoon. Arrange the wings in a single layer evenly over the baking dishes—don't allow the wings to touch each other.

Bake for 35–40 minutes, turning the wings a couple of times during the cooking, or until dark golden brown, and cooked through.

To make the sauce, heat the oil in a medium-sized saucepan. Cook the onion and garlic gently for 4 minutes or until softened. Add the remaining ingredients and bring to the boil. Simmer for 10 minutes. Cool and puree in a blender or with a stick blender until smooth.

NOTE: Remove the chicken wing 'tip' yourself or ask your butcher to do it for you as it will only char and burn.

BUFFALO WINGS

Fixing What Went Wrong

The wings were soggy underneath and not crispy all over. **Reason:** The chicken wings may have been sitting in the oil. Drain off the excess oil before baking and turn the wings during cooking.

Burnt and stuck to the bottom of the baking dish. **Reason:** Baking dish not lined with baking paper.

These bites are delicious served as a snack or with salad as a light meal.

CHICKEN AND HOISIN MEATBALLS

Makes about 15
Cooking style: Bake

Equipment: chopping board, cook's knife, can opener, food processor, non-stick deep baking dish, egg flip, baking paper, small jug or bowl, mixing spoon

1 tablespoons sweet chilli sauce
1 tablespoons soy sauce
1 tablespoons hoisin sauce
1 lime, finely grated rind
4 scallions/spring onions, very roughly chopped
2 cloves garlic, peeled
1 stick celery, very roughly chopped
1¼ in/3 cm knob ginger, peeled, roughly chopped
1 small bunch cilantro/ coriander, washed and roughly chopped
1 lb/500 g free range chicken thigh fillets, very well chilled and cut into large pieces
½ cup canned water chestnuts, drained
1 egg yolk
soy sauce, to serve

Preheat the oven to 420°F/220°C. Line a deep baking dish with baking paper.

Combine the sauces and lime rind in a small bowl or jug.

Place the scallions, garlic, celery, ginger and coriander into a food processor. Pulse briefly until very roughly chopped. Turn to high speed and quickly drop the chilled chicken, water chestnuts and the egg yolk down the chute. Add the sauce mix and pulse until combined. Don't over process, it's nice to leave a little texture to these meatballs.

Using wet hands, roll the mixture into small balls and place into the baking dish. Bake for 15 minutes, then gently turn the balls over. Cook for a further 7 minutes or until dark golden brown and cooked through.

Serve drizzled with extra soy sauce.

NOTE: Be sure to chill the chicken very well before mincing in the processor. This will help it to process or mince more evenly.

• •

Fixing What Went Wrong

The balls fell apart. **Reason:** Not processed enough. The mixture must be 'sticky'

The colour of the meatballs is pale. **Reason:** The oven may not have been on a high enough temperature. It needs to be a very hot oven to seal the balls and achieve a great colour.

Empanadas are golden little Spanish-style pastries. Green olives are a must with the chicken and cheese! If you would like to make your own shortcrust pastry instead, see the Hot Water Pastry recipe (p. 100).

Makes about 16
Cooking style: Bake

Equipment: chopping board, cook's knife, non-stick frying pan, spatula, wooden spoon, mixing bowl, scales, grater, measuring spoons, small bowl, fork, pastry brush, 10 cm round pastry cutter, 2 baking sheets, baking paper

2 tablespoons olive oil
4 oz/120 g free range chicken mince
2 cloves garlic, finely chopped
1¾ oz/50 g piece ham, finely diced (or you can use chorizo sausage)
1¾ oz/50 g cheddar cheese, grated
1¾ oz/50 g pitted green olives
salt flakes and freshly ground black pepper
3 sheets ready rolled frozen puff pastry (good-quality butter puff pastry)
1 large egg yolk, lightly beaten

Preheat the oven to 420°F/220°C (400°F/200°C fan-forced). Line two baking sheets with baking paper.

Heat the oil in a non-stick frying pan, add the chicken mince and garlic and cook, stirring often to break up the lumps. Remove the chicken from pan and place in the mixing bowl. Set aside to cool.

Add the ham, cheese, olives to the chicken mixture and season with plenty of salt and pepper. Mix well to combine.

Lay one sheet of the pastry on a dry surface. Allow the pastry to defrost for 2–3 minutes (just so it can be cut easily—don't let it get too soft or it will be hard to work with).

Cut 5 rounds of pastry from each sheet using a pastry cutter. Place about 1 tablespoon of filling into each round, fold up the sides and crimp the edges together firmly to seal.

Place on the baking sheets leaving a little space in between them to puff as they cook. Using a pastry brush, brush very lightly with the beaten egg yolk. Bake for 10 minutes, reduce the oven temp to 190°C and bake for a further 10 minutes or until golden brown and crisp.

Serve immediately.

NOTE: Make sure the filling is dry, no moisture at all. You can make your own chicken mince in the food processor; for best results make sure the chicken is very well chilled.

CHICKEN, HAM AND OLIVE EMPANADAS

• •

Fixing What Went Wrong

The parcels have opened during the baking. **Reason:** The parcels were overfilled or the edges were not crimped firmly enough.

The pastry is over-cooked and burnt. **Reason:** The temperature wasn't reduced during the baking time. Bake the empanadas for the first 10 minutes at 420°F/220°C to puff up the pastry, then the temperature must be reduced.

This is my version of a delicious lightly spiced Vietnamese favourite. The chicken is cooked before being deep-fried.

VIETNAMESE FRIED CHICKEN

Serves 4
Cooking style: Deep-fry
Other suitable cuts: wings

Equipment: chopping board, cook's knife, 2 large saucepans (one for simmering and one for deep-frying), slotted spoon, colander, thermometer, tongs, rack or large plate lined with paper towel, large sheet of foil to cover

3.5 lb/1.6 kg free range mixed chicken pieces (or cut a size 16 chicken into pieces)
2 teaspoons salt flakes
2 teaspoons Chinese five spice powder
70 fl oz/2 litres (8 cups) vegetable oil for deep-frying
extra salt and lemon wedges for serving

Put the chicken pieces in a large saucepan and cover with cold water. Add the salt and spice powder. Bring to the boil, then reduce the temperature and simmer for 35 minutes (do not boil). As any scum comes to the surface, skim it off with the slotted spoon and discard.

Drain the chicken into the colander (discarding all the cooking water). Allow the chicken to cool.

Use paper towel to pat the chicken dry (there must be no moisture at all on the chicken). Place into a large bowl, sprinkle with the salt and five-spice and toss well.

Divide the chicken into three batches.

Pour the oil into the large saucepan (or deep-fryer). Heat to 400°F/200°C. Use a thermometer to check the temperature or test with a few breadcrumbs—if they sizzle it is ready. Add several pieces of chicken (don't overcrowd the pan) and deep-fry for 5 minutes or until golden. Use tongs to remove each piece of chicken and place on a rack or a plate lined with paper towel. Lightly cover the plate with the foil to keep the chicken warm.

Reheat the oil and cook the remaining batches. Serve immediately with the lemon wedges.

NOTE: Be sure to cook (simmer) the chicken before deep-frying—this is the secret to this recipe—the chicken is cooked twice.

Use a small deep-fryer instead of the saucepan if desired.

Fixing What Went Wrong

The chicken is pale and not crisp. **Reason:** The chicken hasn't been patted dry properly. Any moisture left on the chicken will limit the crisping and browning.

The chicken is soggy. **Reason:** The oil was not hot enough—the oil temperature must be 400°F/200°C when you add the chicken.

Some deep-fried, crispy, golden chicken pieces in a light fluffy batter—yes please!

Serves 4
Cooking style: Deep-fry

Equipment: medium mixing bowl, whisk, chopping board, cook's knife, large deep saucepan or deep-fryer, thermometer, slotted spoon or tongs, 2 plates, paper towel

2 large free-range chicken breast fillets, skin removed
2 egg whites, at room temperature
4 tablespoons cornstarch/ cornflour
70 fl oz/2 litres vegetable oil
salt flakes
freshly ground black pepper
2 fresh chillies, seeded and finely chopped

Pat the chicken dry with paper towel. Cut the chicken into thin strips (about 2.75 in/7 cm long and 1 in/2 cm thick). Divide into two even batches and place on a plate.

Place the egg white and cornflour into a medium-sized bowl and whisk together until a smooth, foamy mixture forms.

Fill the saucepan to no more than half full with clean vegetable oil (or follow instructions if using a deep fryer).

Heat the oil over a medium heat to 370°F/190°C and test with a thermometer or sprinkle in a few little cubes of bread to the oil. If the oil sizzles it is ready. Remove the bread and discard.

Re-whisk the egg mixture a little. Place about half of the chicken into the bowl and coat well in the foamy mixture, making sure each piece is coated well.

Remove with the slotted spoon or tongs, lightly draining away the excess mixture.

Add the chicken pieces to the oil separately, so they don't clump together. Fry for about 4–5 minutes or until the strips are golden and crispy. Remove from the oil and place on the second plate lined with paper towel to drain.

Repeat with the next batch of chicken. For best results, cook small batches at a time.

Sprinkle the cooked crispy chicken with plenty of salt, pepper and the chilli and toss. Serve immediately.

NOTE: Always use a very sharp knife as it will make the cutting easier. Cut the chicken strips into even sized pieces, so they cook evenly. If using a deep-fryer, you may be able to cook larger quantities at once.

CHICKEN WITH CHILLI AND SPICED SALT

· ·

Fixing What Went Wrong

The chicken is oily. **Reason:** The oil was too cold—check the temperature with a thermometer and reheat between batches.

The chicken was dry. **Reason:** The chicken was over-cooked. The fillets are very lean and the cooking time should be quite quick.

The seasoning I have used here is a paste available in 'squeeze' tubes or similar in the fresh food section of the supermarket. You can vary the seasoning for these easy golden brown crispy rolls. Use whatever spice mix or paste you prefer. If you would like to make your own shortcrust pastry, see Hot Water Pastry recipe (p. 100).

EASY SAUSAGE ROLLS

Makes 8 standard-sized sausage rolls
Cooking style: Bake

Equipment: chopping board, cook's knife, small bowl, fork, pastry brush, baking trays lined with baking paper

1 lb/500 g free-range
    chicken thigh fillets, well
    chilled, roughly chopped
4 scallions/spring onions,
    tips discarded, roughly
    chopped
2 tablespoons prepared
    fresh Moroccan or Thai
    seasoning
2 sheets good-quality
    prepared frozen puff
    pastry (butter puff is the
    best)
4 slices seeded bread,
    roughly torn
salt flakes and freshly
    ground black pepper
2 eggs, lightly whisked (or
    use olive oil spray)
2 teaspoons sesame seeds
    (optional)

Preheat the oven to 420°F/220°C. Line 2 baking trays with baking paper.

Place the chicken, scallions, seasoning mix and bread into a food processor. Process until well chopped, but not too fine (leave some texture).

Lay one sheet of the pastry on a dry surface. Allow the pastry to defrost for 2–3 minutes (just so it can be cut easily—don't let it get too soft or it will be hard to work with).

Place the mince mixture (using clean, wet hands to shape) into a 10 in/25 cm log along the edge of the pastry (leave a 1 in/2 cm border around the edge).

Roll up the pastry to enclose the filling (be firm yet gentle to keep a nice even shape). Use your fingertips to seal the pastry together.

Cut the pastry log in half and half again and place each roll, seam side down,

on the lined baking tray. Repeat with the remaining chicken mixture and pastry.

Brush the rolls lightly with the egg yolk or olive oil and sprinkle over the sesame seeds (if using).

Bake for 20–25 minutes or until puffed and golden.

NOTE: Don't thaw the pastry too much as it is difficult to use if softened—it gets very droopy.

Fixing What Went Wrong

The filling has seeped out. **Reason:** The rolls were either overfilled with mixture, or the underneath seam was not firmly (yet gently) pushed together.

The base of the roll is soggy. **Reason:** The oven temperature wasn't hot enough—it must be hot!

We all love a party pie. Who can ever stop at just one? These ones are tiny little mouthfuls so you can enjoy a few more than usual! If you would like to make your own shortcrust pastry instead see Hot Water Pastry recipe (p. 100).

Makes 24 tiny pies
Cooking style: Bake

Equipment: chopping board, cook's knife, scales, large deep non-stick frying pan, spatula, fork, mini-muffin pan, pastry cutters—7 cm and 5.5 cm, baking tray, teaspoon

2 tablespoons olive oil
1 large onion, finely chopped
2 sticks celery, strings removed, finely sliced
3 rashers bacon, finely chopped
1 clove garlic, finely chopped
1 lb/500 g free-range chicken thigh fillets, cut into small pieces (small dice)
3½ fl oz/100 ml white wine
5 fl oz/150 ml chicken stock
2 sprigs each fresh basil and oregano, finely chopped
2 large ripe tomatoes, finely diced
salt and freshly ground black pepper, to taste
4 sheets good-quality prepared frozen shortcrust pastry
1 egg yolk, lightly beaten
3½ oz/100 g butter, for greasing

Heat the oil in the frying pan. Add the onion, celery, bacon and garlic and cook over a medium heat, stirring regularly, for 5 minutes or until softened.

Add the chicken and brown, breaking it up with a fork to remove any lumps. Add about half the wine and allow to evaporate then stir in the remaining wine and again allow to evaporate. Add the stock, fresh herbs, tomato and season well with plenty of salt and pepper.

Simmer for 30 minutes, uncovered, stirring occasionally until the chicken is tender and the mixture has reduced and thickened. Remove from the heat and set aside to cool.

Preheat the oven to 350°F/180°C. Place the baking tray into the oven to heat. Grease your 24 mini-muffin holes well with butter.

Lay one sheet of the pastry onto a dry surface. Allow the pastry to defrost for 2–3 minutes (just so it can be cut easily, don't let it get too soft or it will be hard to work with). Using a 3 in/7 cm cutter, cut out 24 little rounds of pastry from each sheet. Then cut out 24 rounds with a 2 in/5.5 cm cutter.

Carefully put the larger pastry circles into the muffin holes to form a little cup (the pastry needs to come just up above the tin). Use a teaspoon to add the chicken filling (just to the top—don't overfill). Hold a small pastry round in your hand and gently dampen the edges with a little water. Place on top of a filled bottom and gently pinch to seal the edges together. Repeat with the remaining pastry and filling.

Brush the tops with a little of the egg yolk. Place the muffin tray onto the hot baking tray and bake for 20–25 minutes or until golden brown. Cool for 5 minutes in the tray. Carefully remove the little pies and serve.

NOTE: You can use a larger-sized muffin pan if you like but you will need larger-sized cutters for the base.

LITTLE CHICKEN AND BACON PIES

• •

Fixing What Went Wrong

The pie has stuck. **Reason:** The muffin tin wasn't greased. Even if the tin is non-stick it is worth greasing as well.

The filling has seeped out. **Reason:** Too much filling in the pie. Take care to not overfill and make sure the edges are sealed.

MY FAVOURITE CHICKEN SANDWICH

Makes 8 large sandwiches (halved or quartered)
Cooking style: Poach

Equipment: chopping board, cook's knife, large deep non-stick frying pan, tongs, plate, baking tray/slide, large mixing bowl, wooden spoon or spatula, bread and butter knife, serrated knife, food processor

4 free-range chicken whole breast fillets
salt flakes and freshly ground black pepper
3½ oz/100 g slivered almonds
3½ oz/100 g pistachio or macadamia nuts
2 cups good-quality mayonnaise (see recipe below)
2 tablespoons sour cream
2 lemons, finely grated rind
2 sticks celery, thinly sliced
3 scallions/spring onions, ends discarded, very finely sliced (use the white and green sections)
thick sliced white bread, crusts on (like a firm sourdough)
2 oz/60 g butter, softened to room temperature
fresh soft lettuce leaves (such as butter lettuce)

Homemade mayonnaise
1 whole large free range egg and 3 egg yolks (all at room temperature)
10½ fl oz/300 ml safflower or light vegetable oil
pinch superfine/caster sugar
2 teaspoons white vinegar

Preheat the oven to 350°F/180°C.

Place the chicken in a large frying pan. Cover with cold water. Season well with salt and pepper. Bring to a gentle boil, then reduce the heat to low and simmer very gently for 7 minutes or until the chicken is just cooked. Remove the chicken and discard the liquid. Set chicken aside to cool.

Place the nuts on a baking tray and bake for 8 minutes or until golden. Roughly chop and set aside.

Place the mayonnaise, sour cream, lemon rind in the mixing bowl and season well with salt and pepper.

Slice the chicken into thin strips or shred into thin pieces and add to the mixing bowl. Add the nuts, celery and scallions. Mix well.

Lay the bread onto a chopping board, spread with the butter. Top one slice of the bread with a few soft lettuce leaves and a decent mound of the chicken filling. Gently spread over the sandwich and place a slice of bread onto. Repeat with the remaining ingredients. Cut the sandwiches into halves or quarters.

Make the mayonnaise using the food processor (a small bowl option is good here), place the whole egg and yolks into the processor. With the motor running, very very slowly add the oil down the chute. Continue adding the oil until the mixture begins to thicken. Once the mayonnaise is thickening, add the oil in larger amounts and continue mixing and adding the oil to a thick mayonnaise. Add the sugar, vinegar and season well with salt and pepper to taste.

Note: Cook the chicken gently to ensure it's very tender. Make the mayonnaise and store in a sealed container in the refrigerator for up to 5 days.

Fixing What Went Wrong

The bread is soggy. **Reason:** The filling is too wet. This is often because the mayonnaise is too thin—you need a mayonnaise with some body. If making homemade, be sure to drip the oil in drop by drop to ensure it thickens.

The sandwiches are falling apart. **Reason:** Too much filling or flimsy bread. Choose a good strong bread, sourdough is excellent.

The parmesan crust here is just delicious! A food processor is really a must for this recipe.

Serves 4
Cooking style: Deep-fry

Equipment: chopping board, large cook's knife, food processor, measuring jug, 3 deep soup style bowls, large deep frying pan or saucepan, thermometer, tongs or slotted spoon, 2 large plates, paper towel

9 oz/250 g parmesan cheese, roughly chopped
7 oz/200 g (about 7 slices) day old bread, roughly torn
2 cups (9 oz/250 g) all-purpose/plain flour
2 teaspoons salt flakes and freshly ground black pepper
3 large free-range eggs, at room temperature, lightly whisked
1 lb/500 g free-range chicken fillets, cut into long strips
44 fl oz/1.2 litres vegetable oil (sunflower, corn or peanut)

Place the cheese into a food processor and process until finely chopped. Remove and place in one of the soup bowls. Set aside. Add the bread to the food processor and process to fine crumbs. Add the breadcrumbs to the cheese and gently combine using your fingers or a spoon.

Place the flour, salt and pepper into another bowl and gently combine.

Whisk the eggs into the last bowl.

Pat the chicken strips dry with paper towel.

Coat each piece of chicken in the flour, shaking off any excess. Dip into the egg wash then roll each piece in the crumb mixture, pressing the coating onto the chicken with your fingers.

Place the crumbed chicken onto a clean plate lined with paper towel. Refrigerate for at least 30 minutes for the crumbing to firm up.

Fill a pan with the oil (it should be no more than one-third full). Heat over a medium heat until the oil temperature is 400°F/200°C. Use a thermometer or test with a few breadcrumbs—they will sizzle if the oil is hot enough.

Add several pieces of chicken to the oil (don't over-crowd the pan) and fry about 3 minutes or until golden brown. Remove with tongs or slotted spoon and lay cooked chicken on a clean plate lined with paper towel as you go. Repeat with the remaining chicken.

NOTE: When crumbing, try to work with one hand to keep the other clean for other jobs—this makes the process much easier!

PARMESAN CRUSTED CHICKEN STRIPS

Fixing What Went Wrong

The crumbing has fallen off. **Reason:** Chicken hasn't been coated evenly in the egg mixture, which helps the crumbs to stick. Also make sure the crumbs are very fine and that the chicken pieces are allowed to firm up in the fridge before cooking.

The pieces are oily. **Reason:** The temperature of the oil may be too low. This will make the crumbing oily.

Sticky wings are irresistible! Be sure to serve them with finger bowls of water or a
damp cloth as eating these with your fingers is simply a must.

Serves 4
Cooking style: Baked

Equipment: chopping board, cook's knife or cleaver, fine grater, measuring spoons, large mixing bowl, slotted spoon, large baking dish, tongs, baking paper, plastic wrap

3 lb 5 oz/1.5 kg free-range chicken wings
3 tablespoons brown sugar
2 tablespoons honey
3 tablespoons soy sauce
3 tablespoons tomato sauce
2 tablespoons hoisin sauce
2 in/4 cm fresh ginger, peeled, finely grated
2 tablespoons vegetable oil (or peanut, soy, sunflower)
1 clove garlic, finely chopped or grated
1 teaspoon Chinese five spice powder
salt and pepper to taste

Preheat the oven to 400°F/200°C (370°F/190°C fan-forced). Line the base and sides of a large baking dish with baking paper.

Using a large knife or cleaver, cut off the wing tip, just on the middle joint and discard.

Combine all remaining ingredients in the large mixing bowl and stir well.

Add the wings and mix well. (I do this with my clean hands to make sure they are coated well.)

Cover with plastic wrap and refrigerate for 30 minutes to marinate (or longer if time allows). Drain off any excess marinade using the slotted spoon.

Spread the wings evenly over the baking dish—don't allow the wings to touch each other. If too crowded use two baking dishes.

Bake for 35–40 minutes, turning the wings a few times during the cooking, until golden brown, cooked through and very sticky!

STICKY FINGER CHICKEN WINGS

NOTES: Warm the honey to ensure it mixes into the sauce ingredients easily.

Remove the chicken wing tip yourself or ask your butcher to do it for you, as it will only char and burn.

• •

Fixing What Went Wrong

The wings burnt and stuck to the baking dish. **Reason:** The baking dish wasn't properly lined with baking paper.

The wings were over-cooked and stuck together in a lump. **Reason:** The baking dish was overcrowded. Spread out the wings evenly and use two baking dishes if necessary.

These snacks of poached strips of chicken, layered with crisp crunchy lettuce and fresh herbs, rolled in softened rice papers are a texture sensation.

CHICKEN RICE PAPER ROLLS

Serves 4
Cooking style: Poach

Equipment: chopping board, cook's knife, vegetable peeler, large deep frying pan, tongs, measuring jug, scales, 2 large plates, small bowl, pastry brush, food processor with blade, shredding and slicing disks (or box grater)

2 large free-range chicken fillets, tenderloin separated
9 fl oz/250 ml chicken stock or water
1 large carrot, peeled
5 lettuce leaves, washed and refrigerated until use
6 scallions/spring onions, ends trimmed and discarded
2 oz/60 g peanuts, roasted
½ bunch cilantro/ coriander, well washed, leaves picked
1 bunch basil, leaves picked
12 medium dried rice paper rolls
sweet chilli sauce, to serve

Place the chicken fillets and tenderloin into a frying pan and pour over the stock. Bring to a gentle simmer (you will see several small bubbles appearing occasionally, but don't boil) and cook for 4 minutes. Remove the tenderloins if cooked through. Gently turn the fillets over and cook for a further 3–4 minutes or until the chicken is cooked through. Remove from the stock and allow to cool. Once cool, cut into long slices and then shred (I do this with my fingers).

Grate the carrot. Set aside on a plate. Shred the lettuce (using the slicing blade of the food processor or with a knife).

Finely slice the scallions (using the processor or by hand). Place beside the other vegetables. Roughly chop the peanuts (using the processor or by hand).

Lay one sheet of the dried rice paper on a clean plate, moisten it all over with the pastry brush (don't drown it). Wait a few minutes for it to soften. Place another dried sheet on top, again moisten with the water and wait a few minutes. Repeat with the remaining wrappers. You will end up with a stack of softened wrappers. They will not stick together when moistened.

To make the rolls, place one dampened rice paper on the chopping board. Lay on a few herbs, a scattering of nuts, some spring onion and carrot, a few strips of chicken and a little lettuce. Don't add too much filling or it will be difficult to roll up.

Gently fold in the sides over the filling and carefully but firmly roll up the moistened rice paper. Make sure the end piece is moist so it seals. Place seam side down on a clean plate. Repeat with the remaining ingredients.

Serve with your choice of dipping sauces.

NOTES: Don't drown the rice paper with too much water, it needs just enough to moisten. Have all the ingredients ready to go before you start to make the rolls.

Fixing What Went Wrong

The chicken is tough. **Reason:** The chicken was boiled not poached. Cook gently.

The rolls are falling apart. **Reason:** The filling is too chunky or there is too much filling. Fold in the edges and roll up firmly, placing seam side down.

This is perfect for a barbecue or party. Serve with a crisp salad and double or triple the recipe as desired.

Serves 4
Cooking style: Char-grill

Equipment: chopping board, cook's knife, vegetable peeler, measuring spoons, spice mill or mortar and pestle, small frying pan, mixing bowl, large deep dish, wooden or metal skewers, char grill pan, tongs, small saucepan, spatula or wooden spoon

Satay Rub
3 teaspoons cumin seeds
2 teaspoons coriander seeds
2 teaspoons fennel seeds
1 lb/500g free-range chicken thigh fillets, cut into bite-sized pieces (not too small)
2 teaspoons ground turmeric
2 teaspoons brown sugar
2 in/5 cm fresh ginger, peeled
2 stalks fresh lemongrass, white section only, outside leaves peeled, finely chopped
2 cloves garlic, finely chopped
2 tablespoons vegetable oil, for coating before cooking

Quick Peanut Sauce
¾ cup crunchy peanut butter
2 tablespoons sweet chilli sauce
4 fl oz/125 ml cup coconut milk
2 teaspoons soy sauce

Place the cumin, coriander and fennel seeds in a small frying pan and cook gently over a low heat for 3 minutes shaking the pan regularly until very fragrant (don't burn!).

Place the spices into a spice mill or mortar and pestle and grind to a fine powder. Place the chicken into the large mixing bowl with the toasted spices and add turmeric, brown sugar, ginger, lemongrass and garlic. Mix well (I do this with clean hands). Cover with plastic wrap and refrigerate for 1 hour or overnight (if time allows). While the chicken is marinating, soak the wooden skewers (disregard if using metal skewers) in cold water for 30 minutes to prevent them burning.

Thread the chicken onto the skewers.

Heat the char-grill pan over a medium heat until hot. Drizzle the skewers very lightly with oil, rubbing it over the chicken meat.

Place onto the hot grill and cook for about 7 minutes, turning the skewers during the cooking.

Meanwhile, put all the peanut sauce ingredients in the small saucepan. Stir to combine and bring to the boil over a low heat, stirring constantly until the sauce is thick and glossy. Set aside.

NOTES: Whole spices give a superior flavour; however, ground spices can be substituted.
Use your barbecue in place of the char-grill pan if preferred.

SATAY CHICKEN SKEWERS

Fixing What Went Wrong

The flavour is bitter. **Reason:** The spices were burnt while toasting; they only need to be warmed until fragrant.

The chicken skewers stuck to the grill. **Reason:** Skewers were not lightly oiled prior to cooking or they were turned too early—allow the chicken to seal before turning.

SALADS

The classic everyone will always eat. Try my version with a touch of maple syrup and chilli. Have all the ingredients ready and waiting to arrange and dress the salad just before serving.

Serves 4
Cooking style: Barbecue/char-grill

Equipment: chopping board, cook's knife, food processor, measuring jug and measuring spoons, tongs, barbecue plate or char-grill pan

3 thick slices sourdough bread, cut into cubes
4 free-range chicken breast fillets, trimmed to an even thickness (remove the tenderloin and cook separately if desired)
2 tablespoons olive oil
3 tablespoons maple syrup
1 red chilli, very finely chopped
3 rashers smoky bacon, fat trimmed
2 firm Cos lettuce, leaves trimmed and cut in half lengthwise, well washed and dried (see Note)
1 cup parmesan, shredded
½ bunch chives, finely chopped
extra anchovies, for serving

Dressing
2 large egg yolks (from 2 oz/60 g eggs)
1 clove garlic, roughly chopped
pinch salt flakes
ground black pepper
7 fl oz/200 ml olive oil (extra virgin, pure or light)
juice and zest of 1 lemon
2 tablespoons red wine vinegar
1–2 anchovies, plus extra if you love them
extra 1¾–3 ½ fl oz/50–100 ml iced water, to thin the sauce if desired

Start by making the dressing. Place the egg yolks, garlic, salt and pepper into the small bowl of a food processor. With the motor running add the oil very slowly (drip by drip) and continue to process until the mixture starts to thicken. Once thickening, the oil can be added in a slow but steady stream. Add the vinegar, anchovies and water and process until combined. If you want a thinner consistency, add the iced water to thin as required. Chill until using.

Preheat the oven to 400°F/200°C. Line a baking sheet with baking paper. Arrange the bread over the tray in a single layer. Bake for about 12 minutes or until golden brown, turning once during the cooking. Remove and set aside.

Smear the chicken (and tenderloins if using) with the oil, maple syrup and chilli. Preheat a barbecue or char-grill pan until hot. Add the fillets, sear one side for 3–4 minutes, then turn over and cook for a further 5 minutes or until cooked through (the tenderloin will cook in 4–5 minutes total). The chicken will feel firm but a little springy—don't over-cook.

Remove from the grill and let it stand for 5 minutes then thinly slice (I like to slice on a diagonal).

Meanwhile, add the bacon to the hot plate or pan and cook, turning regularly, until very crisp. Allow to cool then crumble into big shards.

To serve, arrange the crisp lettuce over a large platter. Drizzle with a touch of dressing then scatter over bread cubes, bacon, parmesan and a little more dressing. Continue with layers and finish with fresh chives and extra anchovies. Serve immediately.

NOTE: The lettuce must be super crisp. Wash, dry, trim and refrigerate in a sealed container or bag until serving.

CAESAR SALAD WITH MAPLE CHILLI-GLAZED CHICKEN

Fixing What Went Wrong

Soggy salad without crunch? **Reason:** The lettuce wasn't prepped properly. Dry it well before dressing. Don't dress the salad until ready to serve and remember dress it—don't drown it!

Dressing without a tang? **Reason:** You forgot the anchovies. They are super essential to a Caesar salad. You don't need to add extra to the salad but must have them in the dressing for the oomph!

Freekeh is a green wheat (it's also lightly smoked), which has again become popular. It is used like a burghul/cracked wheat. It has a cooking time similar to brown rice.

CHICKEN AND FREEKEH SALAD

Serves 6–8
Cooking style: Barbecue/char-grill
Other cuts suitable: drumsticks

Equipment: chopping board, cook's knife, scissors, baking tray, large saucepan with lid, colander, baking tray, barbecue char-grill or char-grill pan, tongs, food processor,

10½ oz/300 g (1½ cups) freekeh (sold at health food stores and specialty food stores)
2 lb 4 oz/1 kg chicken wings
3½ oz/100 g blanched almonds
5 fl oz/150 ml olive oil
2 lemons, juice and finely grated rind
salt flakes and freshly ground black pepper
6 scallions/spring onions, green tops discarded
1 small bunch flat-leaf parsley/continental parsley, washed
½ bunch of mint, stalks trimmed and discarded, washed
9 oz/250 g cherry tomatoes, halved

Bring a large saucepan of salted water to the boil. Add the freekeh and cook partially covered with the lid, for about 35 minutes or until tender. Drain well into a colander and let cool.

Meanwhile, preheat the oven to 400°F/200°C (350°F/180°C fan-forced). Place the nuts on the tray and roast for 8 minutes or until golden. Allow to cool.

Using a knife or scissors, trim the end tip off the wings and discard. Place the wings, about 1¾ fl oz/50 ml of the oil and half of the lemon rind into the mixing bowl and toss well. Preheat the barbecue char-grill or char-grill pan until hot. Place the wings on the grill and cook over a medium heat, turning often for 8–10 minutes or until golden brown and cooked. Remove and set aside to keep warm.

Place the nuts into a food processor and roughly chop (or hand chop). Remove and set aside. Add the scallions, parsley and mint and chop (or chop by hand).

While the freekeh is still a little warm (or at room temperature), toss together the remaining oil, lemon rind, lemon juice, herbs, chicken wings and tomato halves. Arrange the salad on a large serving platter. Scatter with the toasted nuts and serve.

NOTE: The freekeh has a long cooking time, about 40 minutes. Partially cover with a lid to keep in some moisture and do not boil the pot dry.

Fixing What Went Wrong

The char-grill plate kept flaring. **Reason:** Oil poured directly onto the plate—only coat the chicken in the oil.

The chicken wings are burnt on the outside yet raw inside. **Reason:** The heat was too high. Chicken wings are best turned often during char-grilling.

A Waldorf salad is all about the mayonnaise. The balance between the crisp apples and the crunchy celery is the key. Adding chicken adds the perfect balance and makes this salad a delicious meal.

Serves: 4–6
Cooking style: Poach

Equipment: chopping board, cook's knife, food processor, measuring spoons and cups, tongs, baking tray, non-stick frying pan, small mixing bowl, spatula or wooden spoon, large mixing bowl, colander, vegetable peeler

3 free-range chicken breast fillets, tenderloin removed (use in another recipe)
salt flakes and freshly ground black pepper
3 slices lemon
3½ oz/100 g walnuts
1 cup good-quality mayonnaise (or see recipe below)
½ cup natural yoghurt
2 tablespoons sour cream
1 teaspoon Dijon mustard
1 lemon, finely grated rind and juice
3 medium green apples, halved (I don't bother removing the core)
3 sticks celery, ends trimmed
3 scallions/spring onions, ends trimmed and discarded
7 oz/200 g rocket leaves

Homemade Mayonnaise
1 whole large free-range egg and 3 egg yolks (all at room temperature)
10½ fl oz/300 ml safflower or light vegetable oil
pinch superfine/caster sugar
2 teaspoons white vinegar

To make homemade mayonnaise using the food processor (a small bowl option is good here), place the whole egg and yolks into the processor. With the motor running, very, very slowly add the oil down the chute drip by drip. Continue adding the oil until the mixture begins to thicken. Once the mayonnaise is thickening you can add the oil in larger amounts. Continue mixing and adding the oil until you have a thick mayonnaise. Add the sugar, vinegar and season well with salt and pepper to taste.

Preheat the oven to 350°F/180°C.

Place the chicken in a large non-stick frying pan. Cover with cold water. Season well with salt and pepper and add the lemon slices. Bring to the boil, then reduce the heat to low and simmer very gently for 7 minutes or until the chicken is just cooked. Remove the chicken and discard the stock.

Recipe continued.

CHICKEN WALDORF SALAD

CHICKEN WALDORF SALAD

cont.

Cool the chicken then cut into large bite-sized pieces.

Place the walnuts on a baking tray, bake for 8 minutes or until golden. Roughly chop and set aside.

In a small mixing bowl, combine the mayonnaise, yoghurt, sour cream, mustard, lemon rind and season well with salt and pepper.

Using a food processor (with a thin slicing blade), thinly slice the apples, celery and scallions separately.

Remove from the processor. Place the apples into a large mixing bowl and sprinkle over a little of the lemon juice and toss well (this will prevent the apples discolouring). Add the celery and spring onions.

Add the mayonnaise mixture and chicken, toss well. Add about half the nuts and mix to combine.

To serve, place the rocket on a serving platter and top with the salad. Scatter over the remaining nuts and parsley.

NOTE: Make the mayonnaise and store in a sealed container in the refrigerator for up to 5 days.

Fixing What Went Wrong

The salad is soggy. **Reason:** The salad wasn't served immediately. Make this salad just before serving so the apples stay very crisp. The mayonnaise and chicken can be made and refrigerated up to two days ahead.

The creaminess of the avocado with the tang of the fennel and freshness of the mint is delicious and makes this a vibrant salad, full of crunch.

Serves 4
Cooking style: Char-grill
Other cuts suitable: breast fillets

Equipment: scales, chopping board, cook's knife, measuring cups and spoons, smaller knife, char-grill plate or large frying pan, food processor, small bowl, balloon whisk, large mixing bowl, tongs

2 lb 4 oz/1 kg chicken thigh fillets
2 tablespoons olive oil
2 teaspoons freshly ground black pepper
2 teaspoons salt flakes
2 ripe avocados
2 baby fennels
2 cups baby spinach leaves, washed
4 cups mixed lettuce leaves
½ small bunch mint, leaves picked

Dressing
4 fl oz/120 ml extra virgin olive oil
2 lemons, finely grated rind and juice
2 teaspoons seeded Dijon mustard

Cut the fillets into large pieces. Place into a mixing bowl with the olive oil, pepper and salt. Toss well.

Heat a char grill plate until slightly smoky. Place on the chicken pieces and cook for 2 minutes, turn over and cook for a further 2–3 minutes or until golden brown and the chicken is just cooked. Remove and set aside to rest.

Cut the avocados in half, remove the stone and cut into thick slices. Trim the very end off the fennel and the very outside tougher layer and discard. Trim off the soft fronds and set aside. Slice the bulb and stalks thinly in a food processor (or by hand).

Arrange the lettuce, spinach, fennel slices, mint leaves and avocado over a large platter.

Combine the dressing ingredients in a small bowl, season with salt and pepper and whisk. Drizzle over the salad.

Scatter over the reserved fennel fronds to serve.

PEPPERED CHICKEN, FENNEL, AVOCADO AND MINT SALAD

NOTE: Baby fennel is very tender so only the very base is trimmed and discarded. If a large bulb is used, peel off the harder outside layer and discard.

Fixing What Went Wrong

The chicken is watery and pale. **Reason:** Char-grill is not hot enough. It needs to be hot to sear the chicken.

The fennel has discoloured. **Reason:** Salad hasn't been served straight away. The fennel will start to turn brown, prepare quickly and serve salad straight away (or toss the sliced fennel is a little lemon juice to keep it white).

The texture of the fried bread and crisp vegetables with the chilled chicken is delicious. Serve immediately to keep the crunch.

MEDITERRANEAN CRISPY FLAT BREAD AND GRILLED CHICKEN SALAD

Serves 4
Cooking style: Char-grill
Other cuts suitable: thigh fillets

Equipment: chopping board, cook's knife, large plate, char-grill pan or barbecue, sheet of foil to cover, large frying pan, tongs

4 fl oz/125 ml (½ cup) olive oil
3 teaspoons sweet paprika
2 teaspoons sumac (sold at specialty stores and good supermarkets)
2 cloves garlic, finely chopped
2 large, chicken fillets, skin removed
2 rounds of flat bread, torn into large pieces
2 ripe tomatoes, diced
2 Lebanese cucumbers, diced
1 red and 1 green bell pepper/capsicum, seeds removed and diced
½ small red onion, finely diced
1 bunch mint, well washed, leaves picked and chopped
½ bunch flat-leaf parsley, leaves picked and torn

Dressing
2 tablespoons olive oil
2 lemons, finely grated rind and juice
salt flakes and freshly ground black pepper
little extra sumac, for serving

Smear about 2 tablespoons olive oil, paprika, sumac and garlic all over the chicken (if time allows cover and refrigerate for 30 minutes).

Heat a barbecue hot plate or char-grill pan to hot. Place the chicken (and tenderloins) onto the grill and cook for 3 minutes. Remove the tenderloins and set aside.

Carefully turn the fillets over and cook for a further 4 minutes or until cooked. Remove and set aside on a plate and cover with foil to keep warm. Allow to rest while preparing the salad.

Heat the remaining oil until hot in a large frying pan. Add the bread in batches and shallow fry for 1–2 minutes, or until lightly golden and crisp, turning the bread pieces over in the oil. Remove and drain on paper towel (don't over-crowd the pan).

To serve, slice the chicken. Arrange some of the bread on a large serving plate, top with the chicken, diced tomato, cucumber, capsicum, onion and herbs and then scatter over more of the bread (you can crumble it into smaller pieces). Whisk together the dressing ingredients and drizzle over the salad. Sprinkle with extra sumac.

NOTE: Use any style of flat bread, lavosh bread, spelt or rice flat bread.

Fixing What Went Wrong

The bread is soggy and oily. **Reason:** The oil wasn't hot enough to crisp up the bread.

If you love the flavour and texture of sweet grilled pineapple, creamy avocado and the crunch of corn chips, this salad is for you.

Serves 4
Cooking style: Barbecue/char-grill

Equipment: chopping board, cook's knife, large mixing bowl, smaller mixing bowl, fork, measuring cups and spoons, smaller mixing bowl, char-grill pan or barbecue hot plate, large sheet foil, tongs

2 lb 4 oz/1 kg chicken thigh fillets, cut in half (or into large pieces)
2 red or orange bell pepper/capsicum, halved, membrane and seeds discarded, cut into thick strips
3½ fl oz/100 ml vegetable oil (corn, sunflower or olive)
1 tablespoon sweet paprika
2 teaspoons smoked paprika
¼ teaspoon ground cayenne pepper
¼ teaspoon freshly ground black pepper
4 thick slices fresh pineapple, skin on
juice and zest of 2 limes,
2 large avocado, halved, stone removed and peeled

¼ bunch cilantro/coriander, finely chopped
2 tablespoons sour cream
salt flakes and extra freshly ground black pepper, to taste
1 small iceberg lettuce, washed and very roughly chopped
7 oz/200 g good-quality plain corn chips or tortilla strips

Combine the chicken, bell pepper, oil, spices and pepper in a mixing bowl. Toss well. Cover and refrigerate and marinate for 1 hour (or overnight if time allows).

Heat a barbecue hot plate to smoking hot. Place the chicken and bell pepper pieces on the grill and cook for 3 minutes without moving.

Lay the pineapple on the grill and allow to brown. Squeeze a little of the lime juice over the chicken (it will steam and sizzle).

Cook the chicken and bell pepper for another 4 minutes or until tender, turning often to brown and char nicely on the edges. Turn the pineapple over and brown the other side. Remove the chicken, bell pepper and pineapple from the grill and keep warm.

Mash the avocado in a bowl with the cilantro, about 1 tablespoon of lime juice, ½ lime rind, the sour cream and salt and pepper to taste (don't over-mash, keep it rough and rustic).

Cut the pineapple into thick triangles (I like the skin left on, it looks great).

Divide the lettuce into the serving bowls, top with a few corn chips, then some of the chicken, bell pepper and pineapple. Sprinkle over the remaining lime juice and rind and season with salt and pepper. Top with a few more corn chips and dollop with the avocado mash. Serve immediately.

NOTE: Buy good-quality (or authentic) corn chips/tortilla chips.

MEXICAN SPICED LIME CHICKEN AND PINEAPPLE SALAD

• •

Fixing What Went Wrong

The chicken wasn't seared and nicely charred on the edges. **Reason:** The barbecue/grill plate wasn't hot enough—adding the lime juice creates moisture and the sugars in the limes help the edges to caramelise.

The corn chips went soggy. **Reason:** Be sure to assemble and serve immediately. This salad doesn't 'stand' well. Make, serve and eat.

This is one of my favourite salads. Shred the chicken into lovely long pieces and be sure to add plenty of mint.

VIETNAMESE CHICKEN SALAD

Serves 4–6
Cooking style: Poach

Equipment: chopping board, cook's knife, food processor with thin slicing disc, large frying pan, large mixing bowl, smaller mixing bowl, tongs

3 large chicken breast fillets, tenderloin section separated (the tenderloin will cook a little quicker than the rest of the flesh)
24 fl oz/700 ml water
sea salt flakes
lots of freshly ground black pepper

Marinade
1 small red onion, peeled
4 fl oz/120 ml rice wine or white wine vinegar
1¾ oz/50 g white sugar
2 teaspoons sea salt
7 oz/200 g very fresh Chinese cabbage
2 medium carrots, peeled
1 cup each of mint and basil (around ½ bunch)
1½ fl oz/40 ml vegetable oil (sunflower or peanut oil)
juice of 1 lime
1¾ oz/50 g peanuts, toasted and chopped
2 tablespoons fried shallots

Put the chicken into a frying pan in a single layer, cover with cold water and season well with salt and pepper. Bring to a very gentle simmer (little tiny bubbles will appear) and cook uncovered for 8 minutes or until the chicken is tender (do not overcook). Remove from the poaching liquid and allow to cool.

Meanwhile, very finely slice the onion. Pop the onion into a large mixing bowl with the vinegar, sugar and salt. Toss well. Allow to marinate while the chicken is cooking and you are preparing the rest of the vegetables.

Finely shred the cabbage and carrot (you can do this in a food processor). Set aside. Chop the mint and basil.

Using a sharp knife, thinly slice the chicken breast into long strips and then shred (I use my fingers to shred). Combine the chicken, cabbage, carrot and onion mixture, about ¾ of the herbs, the oil and lime juice. Toss well.

Arrange over a large platter or in a large bowl and scatter over the remaining herbs, peanuts and fried shallots. Serve immediately.

NOTE: Use Chinese cabbage for the best texture. If not available, a Savoy cabbage is the next best choice. Fried shallots are sold in Asian food stores and some larger supermarkets in the Asian foods section.

Fixing What Went Wrong

The chicken was not silky and soft. **Reason:** The poaching was too rough—the chicken should be very gently simmered.

The salad was soggy. **Reason:** The salad was not served immediately. This salad is best tossed then served immediately. The vegetables and chicken can be prepared earlier, but kept separate.

The bite of the ginger marries so well with the divine sweetness of the mango and soft silky slices of poached chicken. This is a simple recipe relying on gentle poaching and delicate flavours.

SILKY CHICKEN, MANGO AND GINGER SALAD

Serves 4
Cooking style: Poach

Equipment: chopping board, cook's knife, scales, vegetable peeler, tongs, heavy based large frying pan, measuring jug, fine grater

3 cups (1.6 pints/750 ml) chicken stock
3 sprigs of cilantro/coriander with stalks chopped, and leaves picked
2 thick slices fresh ginger
2 large skinless chicken breasts fillets, tenderloin trimmed and set aside
1 ripe mango, cut into large strips
3 scallions/spring onions, finely sliced diagonally
1¾ oz/50 g (about ¼ bunch) coriander, leaves and stalks separated, for serving
2 in/5 cm ginger, peeled and very finely sliced, for serving
1 clove garlic, peeled, and very finely sliced
¼ cup coconut vinegar or white wine vinegar
sea salt and fresh ground black pepper
3½ oz/100 g baby spinach leaves, washed and dried

Pour the chicken stock into the frying pan. Add the coriander stalks, thick ginger slices and then the chicken fillets and tenderloins. The stock needs to cover the chicken.

Bring to a gentle simmer (this means the liquid is very gently cooking without boiling, you will see just a few bubbles). Cook very gently for 3–4 minutes. Remove the smaller tenderloins, setting aside. Turn the fillets over in the poaching liquid and continue to cook for a further 4 minutes, or until cooked through.

Remove the chicken and set aside to cool for about 15 minutes, discarding all the poaching liquid and herbs.

Slice each fillet and the tenderloin into very thin strips, cutting slightly on the diagonal across the fillets (the thinner the better).

To serve, combine the mango, scallions, cilantro leaves, chicken, sliced ginger, garlic, vinegar, salt and pepper. Toss well.

Divide the spinach leaves between the serving bowls. Top with the chicken mixture.

NOTE: Make sure the ginger and garlic are sliced paper thin—this makes all the difference to this salad. The chicken can be sliced and served warm in the salad. Fresh pineapple can also be used.

• •

Fixing What Went Wrong

The chicken was dry. **Reason:** Not 'simmering' the chicken. It must be poached very gently to be silky.
The chicken was flavourless. **Reason:** Not using good stock, not seasoning with fresh herbs or plenty or salt and pepper to balance the flavour.
The salad was soggy. **Reason:** Making the salad and letting it stand. This salad is better tossed and served immediately.

SOUPS

Just like Grandma used to make. Feeling poorly? Need some comfort? This soup fixes everything.

Serves 4–6
Cooking style: Simmer

Equipment: chopping board, cook's knife, vegetable peeler, 2 large saucepans, measuring cups and spoons, wooden spoon, spatula, colander, slotted spoon, tongs, large mixing bowl

Stock
2 sticks celery, sliced
2 large carrots, peeled, ends trimmed, chopped
1 large onion, peeled and chopped
2 bay leaves
4 peppercorns
1 free range, size 16 (3.5 lb/1.6 kg) whole chicken, well rinsed

Soup
2 tablespoons olive oil
2 leeks, ends and green section trimmed, well washed and thinly sliced
2 carrots, peeled
2 sticks celery
1 clove garlic, peeled, finely chopped
½ cup risoni (small shaped rice pasta) or long grain rice
3½ oz/100 g green beans, topped and tailed, cut into 1 in/4 cm pieces
2 cobs corn, husks and silks removed, kernels trimmed from the cob
1 lemon, finely grated rind and juice
sea salt and freshly ground black pepper
½ small bunch parsley, stalks removed, leaves finely chopped

To make the stock, place the celery, carrots, onion, bay leaves, peppercorns and chicken into a large saucepan. Cover with cold water. Bring to the boil over a medium heat. Reduce heat and simmer for 1 hour. Use a slotted spoon to skim off any scum that rises to the surface.

Using tongs, carefully remove the chicken from the stock (tipping out any stock from inside the cavity) and set aside to cool. Return the stock to the boil and simmer for 30 minutes. Place a colander over a large bowl and drain the stock.

Discard the vegetables and keep the precious broth. If desired, the broth can be placed in the fridge and cooled. The fat will rise to the surface and can be skimmed off.

Using gloves (if the chicken is still too warm to comfortably touch), remove the skin and discard. Slice the flesh and shred into long thin pieces. Set aside.

Heat the oil in a clean saucepan. Add the leeks, carrot, celery and garlic. Cook over a medium heat, stirring occasionally, for 8 minutes or until softened and glossy (do not burn).

Add the reserved chicken broth and bring to the boil. Add the risoni pasta or rice and cook for 10 minutes, or until tender. Add the beans and corn and cook for 5 minutes. Finally stir in the shredded chicken, lemon rind and juice and parsley. Season well with salt and pepper.

NOTE: Don't overcook the vegetables—keep them brightly coloured, just tender but with a little texture still left.

CHICKEN SOUP

Fixing What Went Wrong

The soup is gritty and 'dirty'. **Reason:** the scum hasn't been skimmed from the surface of the broth during the simmering.

The soup is oily. **Reason:** Fat hasn't been removed from the stock.

The base of all delicious cooking is good stock. Fresh stock adds that special flavour. Cool before freezing into 9 fl oz/250 ml or 17½ fl oz/500 ml amounts.

GOOD CHICKEN STOCK

Cooking style: Simmer

Equipment: chopping board, cook's knife, very large saucepan, slotted spoon, large colander, large saucepan or bowl

5 lb 8 oz/2.5 kg free-range chicken carcasses, necks or wings
3 large onions, quartered (you can leave the skin on)
3 large carrots, roughly chopped
3 sticks celery, roughly chopped
2 bay leaves, torn
¼ bunch parsley, roughly torn
4 sprigs thyme
6 peppercorns

Place the chicken in a large colander. Rinse well under cold water (this helps to keep the stock clear).

Place all the ingredients in a large saucepan. Cover well with cold water. Place on the heat and bring up to a big boil. Reduce the heat and simmer for 2 hours. Keep topping up the stock with cold water.

Use a slotted spoon to remove the scum and grit that comes to the surface.

Turn off the heat. Place a large colander into a big saucepan or over a large bowl. Drain the stock into the colander reserving the precious liquid.

Refrigerate for up to 5 days. Or freeze in 9 or 17½ fl oz/250 or 500 ml amounts for up to 3 months.

NOTE: Always add cold water to stock. For a darker stock, roast the chicken bones in a baking paper-lined baking dish at 420°F/220°C for 30 minutes then follow the method above.

Fixing What Went Wrong

The stock was cloudy. **Reason:** The chicken wasn't rinsed. And only add cold water to the stock.

The stock was flavourless. **Reason:** Not enough chicken bones used or not simmered for long enough.

This is a quick delicious meal. Serve in huge deep bowls. I'm usually not a lover of pre-made pastes, but laksa pastes are very good. Look for them in the supermarket or Asian food stores.

CHICKEN LAKSA

Serves 4–6
Cooking style: Simmer

Equipment: chopping board, cook's knife, colander, large frying pan, large saucepan, plate, large mixing bowl

10½ oz/300 g dried vermicelli noodles
3 x 1 lb/500 g free-range chicken fillets
1 x 7 oz/200 g jar pre-made laksa paste
26 fl oz/750 ml good chicken stock (buy the best you can find or make your own)
17½ fl oz/500 ml coconut milk
1 fresh red chilli, finely sliced (optional)
5 oz/150 g green beans, diagonally sliced
3½ oz/100 g snow peas, string removed, halved
1 tablespoon grated palm sugar or brown sugar
2 limes, finely grated rind and juice
5 oz/150 g bean sprouts, to serve
lime wedges, to serve
Thai basil, to serve

Place the vermicelli into a large mixing bowl, cover with boiling water and set aside for 5 minutes or until softened and plump. Drain noodles in a colander and set aside.

Place the chicken into the deep frying pan. Cover with cold water and bring to a gentle simmer. Cook for about 7 minutes or until the chicken is cooked through. Remove from the liquid and set aside to cool. Slice very thinly.

Put the laksa paste, chicken stock and coconut milk into a large saucepan. Bring to the boil, stirring. Simmer uncovered for 3 minutes. Add the red chilli (if using) and green beans and cook for 4 minutes. Add the snow peas, palm sugar, lime rind and juice. Cook for 2 minutes.

Divide the noodles between the bowls. Top with the chicken, ladle over lots of coconut broth. Top with bean sprouts and lime wedges. Scatter with basil leaves, just before serving.

NOTE: Soak the noodles until soft but not falling apart.

Fixing What Went Wrong

The chicken is tough. **Reason:** It is overcooked. Poach gently until just tender. Never let the water boil when poaching—just a few small bubbles should gently appear.

The laksa is soggy and lifeless. **Reason:** The laksa was pre-made. The laksa is to be made, served and eaten immediately. You can poach the chicken beforehand and cook the noodles, but heat the broth and serve straight away.

A
HANDFUL
OF
INGREDIENTS

We all love charcoal chicken for the colour, texture and flavour. This recipe is cheating a little as I don't truthfully cook it over hot charcoals—but a hot barbecue with a cover or lid will do the trick.

CHARCOAL CHICKEN

Serves 4
Cooking style: Barbecue

Equipment: chopping board, cook's knife, scissors, kitchen string, tongs, heatproof baking dish for roasting, large rack to place onto the barbecue plate, small rack or trivet to sit in the dish

3.5 lb/1.6 kg (size 16) free-range whole chicken
2 lemons, halved
few sprigs parsley and oregano
1¾ oz/50 g butter, at room temperature
3 tablespoons olive oil
salt flakes and ground white pepper

Rinse the chicken well and pat dry inside and out with paper towel.

Place the large rack onto the barbecue plate. The baking dish will sit on top of this preventing the bottom of the baking dish charring and burning and helping to circulate the heat around the chicken. Preheat the barbecue with the lid down to 480°F/250°C.

Place the small rack or trivet inside the baking dish.

Put 3 lemon halves and herbs inside the chicken cavity. Tuck the wings underneath or trim off the bottom section of the wing using scissors, and discard. Tie the legs together firmly with kitchen string.

Rub the chicken all over with butter using clean hands then drizzle over the olive oil and season well with salt and pepper.

Sit the chicken, breast side down (this is very important), onto the trivet in the pan. Pour about ¼ cup of water into the baking dish.

Working quickly, place the baking dish onto the rack in the hot barbecue. Cover with the hood or lid. Cook for 20 minutes. Reduce the temperature to about 400°F/200°C and cook for a further 20 minutes.

Working quickly, open the cover and turn the chicken over so the breast is facing up (being careful not to pierce the skin with the tongs).

Cover with the lid and cook for a further 30 minutes. Test the chicken with the tip of a knife into the thickest section of the thigh. The juices should run clear. If the juices have a pink tinge, place back into the barbecue and cook for a further 10 minutes.

Remove the chicken and set aside to rest for 15 minutes.

Squeeze over the remaining lemon juice and carve. Serve with potato salad, a tossed garden salad and good bread.

NOTE: Make sure the chicken is washed and patted dry with paper towel before cooking.

Fixing What Went Wrong

The skin was not crispy. **Reason:** Temperature wasn't high enough or the skin wasn't coated in enough butter or oil.

The bottom of the chicken is soggy. **Reason:** The chicken was sitting in juices—always sit on a trivet/rack inside the baking dish.

With a simple combination of flavours, this chicken is baked until the skin is dark golden brown, crispy and delicious.

Serves 4
Cooking style: Baked
Other cuts suitable: use drumsticks

Equipment: chopping board, cook's knife, measuring spoons and cup, large mixing bowl, small mixing bowl, tongs, large baking dish, paper towel, plastic wrap, baking paper.

4 x 10½ oz/300 g free-range chicken Marylands (leg and thigh section)
3 tablespoons olive oil
1 tablespoon ground cumin
2 teaspoons freshly ground black pepper
2½ fl oz/80 ml port (or sweet sherry)
4 bay leaves, torn
1 orange, finely grated rind and juice

Rinse the chicken under cold water, pat dry with paper towel. Lay the pieces in a baking dish.

Combine the olive oil, cumin, pepper, port, bay leaves, and orange rind and juice in a small mixing bowl. Drizzle over the chicken and then, using clean hands, rub and smear the mixture all over the chicken.

Cover with plastic wrap film and refrigerate for at least 1 hour (or overnight if time allows).

Preheat the oven to 400°F/200°C, and line a baking dish with baking paper.

Remove the chicken with the tongs from the marinade, shaking off as much excess liquid as possible. Lay the pieces, skin side up, into the lined baking dish.

Bake for 30 minutes. Reduce the temperature to 350°F/180°C and cook for an additional 10 minutes or until cooked.

Test if the chicken is cooked by piercing the thickest section of the thigh with a knife. The juices should run clear.

ORANGE AND CUMIN ROASTED CHICKEN THIGHS

NOTE: Use fresh or dried bay leaves and remember to remove before serving.

• •

Fixing What Went Wrong

The chicken has stuck to the dish. **Reason:** Not lining the baking dish. You must roast on baking paper as the sugar in the port will lightly caramelise and cause the skin to stick to the dish.

The chicken skin is soggy. **Reason:** Skin not dried before baking. Be sure to pat it dry at the beginning and then make sure the marinade is drained so the chicken doesn't sit in its juices.

This recipe couldn't be easier. Bake covered and then uncovered to crisp and colour.
Serve with bread!

Serves 4
Cooking style: Baked

Equipment: chopping board, cook's knife, measuring spoons and cup, large mixing bowl, tongs, large baking dish, large sheet of foil, paper towel

3.5 lb/1.5 kg free range chicken thigh fillets
3 tablespoons olive oil
3 cloves garlic, finely chopped
1–2 red chillies, finely chopped (remove the seeds for a milder flavour)
2 sprigs rosemary, finely chopped
3½ fl oz/100 ml white wine
6 oz/180 g Kalamata olives
14 oz/400 g truss baby tomatoes, gently removed from the vine
salt flakes and freshly ground black pepper

Pat the chicken dry with paper towel. Place in a mixing bowl with the oil, garlic, chilli and rosemary.

Cover with plastic wrap and refrigerate to marinate for at least one 1 hour (or longer if time permits).

Preheat the oven to 350°F/180°C. Arrange the chicken, white wine and olives in a baking dish.

Bake, uncovered, for 20 minutes. Add the tomatoes, increase the temperature to 410°F/210°F. Bake for another 10 minutes.

Serve this dish all together on a large platter.

CHICKEN ROASTED WITH TOMATOES, OLIVES AND WHITE WINE

NOTE: You can also use green olives.

Fixing What Wont Wrong

The chicken is cooked but not succulent. **Reason:** The chicken is baked uncovered. Be sure to cover with foil for the first half of the cooking

A simple dish, so easily made. Replace the mint with basil or even coriander and diced chilli for a Thai flavour.

PASTA WITH CHICKEN, ZUCCHINI, PEAS AND MINT

Serves 4
Cooking style: Pan-fry

Equipment: chopping board, cook's knife, food processor or box grater, large saucepan with lid, colander, large non-stick frying pan, spatula or wooden spoon

1 lb/500 g dried penne or fusilli pasta
4 medium zucchini, ends trimmed
3 tablespoons olive oil
3 cloves garlic, finely chopped
1 lb/500 g free-range chicken thigh fillets, cut into thin strips
3½ oz/100 g frozen peas, defrosted
5 oz/150 g ricotta cheese
salt and freshly ground black pepper
several mint leaves, finely chopped

Fill the saucepan with water and season well with salt. Bring to a rapid boil. Add the pasta and stir well. Cook for 8 minutes without lid or until just tender. Drain into a colander and reserve about ½ cup of the cooking water. Return the cooked pasta to the saucepan, cover and set aside.

Meanwhile, coarsely grate the zucchini in a food processor (or with a grater). Heat the oil in a frying pan over a high heat. Add the garlic and half of the chicken, toss for 3 minutes or until lightly browned. Remove from the pan. Add the remaining chicken and cook. Return all the chicken to the pan with any juices. Stir through the zucchini and peas, cover and cook for 3 minutes, or until the zucchini just softens.

Add the chicken mixture to the pasta along with the reserved cooking liquid, ricotta and season with plenty of the salt and pepper. Toss gently to combine. Scatter over the mint. Serve immediately.

NOTE: Timing is important with this recipe. While the pasta is cooking, sear the chicken and complete the recipe. You will then only need to toss it all together while the pasta is piping hot.

. . . .

Fixing What Went Wrong

The mixture curdled. **Reason:** The ricotta was cooked. It should just be tossed with the hot ingredients.

A tangy lemon rind and caper freshly chopped gremolata adds life to simple chicken fillets.

Serves 4
Cooking style: Pan-fry
Other suitable cuts: thigh fillets

Equipment: chopping board, cook's knife, vegetable peeler, food processor, large non-stick frying pan with lid, egg flip

4 free-range chicken fillets, tenderloin removed (can be used for another recipe)
9 oz/250 g cherry tomatoes, halved

Gremolata
½ large bunch flat-leaf parsley, stems removed
3 cloves garlic, peeled
1 lemon, cut the rind into strips with a vegetable peeler and juice the lemon
2 tablespoons drained capers
3 tablespoons olive oil
salt flakes and plenty freshly ground black pepper

In a food processor, place the parsley, garlic, lemon rind, capers and 2 tablespoons olive oil. Process until finely chopped.

Spread the chicken fillets thinly on both sides with the gremolata. Heat the frying pan over a medium low heat.

Add the chicken and cook without moving for 3–4 minutes each side, turning only once during the cooking. About half way through the cooking, sprinkle with a little lemon juice—this adds some moisture and helps the chicken cook evenly and stay moist.

Add the tomatoes, cover with the lid and cook for another 2–3 minutes or until cooked through and the tomatoes have split a little.

LEMON AND CAPER GREMOLATA SEARED CHICKEN

NOTE: When peeling the lemon strips, try to not have the white pith on the inside of the zest, as the pith is quite bitter.

Fixing What Went Wrong

The gremolata falls off the chicken. **Reason:** The gremolata was too chunky. Process until fine.

The gremolata is singed and burnt. **Reason:** The pan is too hot and the herb crust has burnt.

Chicken is dry. **Reason:** The chicken has been overcooked. Breast fillets are very lean. Cook until there is still juice and just cooked through. Adding the lemon juice and cooking with the lid on at the end will also help.

CHILLI CHICKEN ROASTED WITH EGGPLANT AND TOMATOES

Serves 4
Cooking style: Pan-fry and bake

Equipment: chopping board, cook's knife, measuring spoons, large heavy-based non-stick frying pan, slotted spoon, tongs, large baking dish, paper towel

1 medium eggplant
2 large red bell pepper/ capsicum
4 medium tomatoes (with the calyx left on)
3 tablespoons olive oil
salt flakes and freshly ground black pepper
4 free-range chicken breast fillets
½ teaspoon chilli flakes
1½ oz/40 g butter, melted

Preheat the oven to 420°F/220°C. Line the base of a heavy-based baking dish with baking paper.

Trim the stem from the eggplant, cut in half and then into long thick wedges. Halve the bell pepper and remove all the membrane and seeds, cut into wedges.

Arrange the eggplant and peppers in a single layer (don't let them touch) in the baking dish. Drizzle with about ¾ of the olive oil and sprinkle liberally with the salt and pepper.

Roast for 20 minutes. Carefully remove the tomatoes (with a slotted spoon, so they don't collapse) and set aside. Return the baking dish to the oven and bake the remaining vegetables for 15 minutes, or until nearly cooked and slightly crisping on the edges.

Pat the chicken fillet dry with a paper towel. Sprinkle with salt flakes, pepper and the chilli.

Add the remaining oil and butter to the frying pan. Heat over a medium heat until hot and the butter is foamy. Add the chicken and cook for 3–4 minutes or until the chicken is golden brown, turn over and cook 2 minutes on the other side.

Remove the baking dish from the oven, return the tomatoes and add the crispy chicken, skin side up, on top of the vegetables. Reduce the oven temperature to 340°F/170°C. Bake for a further 15 minutes or until chicken is cooked through.

NOTE: You can use egg or Roma tomatoes, cut in half lengthwise in place of the whole tomatoes if preferred.

Fixing What Went Wrong

The vegetables are softened and colourless. **Reason:** The oven was not hot enough. The oven must be hot to brown the vegetables and soften them
The chicken skin is not super crispy. **Reason:** The skin was damp before cooking. Make sure you pat dry the skin with paper towel before pan-frying.

You can vary the filling in the middle of this rolled up chicken. I add whatever cheese is on hand or simply use finely diced tomatoes, a few breadcrumbs and some freshly chopped herbs. You can vary the filling in the middle of this rolled up chicken. I add whatever cheese is on hand or simply use finely diced tomatoes, a few breadcrumbs and some freshly chopped herbs.

ROLL IT UP CHICKEN

Serves 4

Cooking style: Pan-fried and baked

Equipment: chopping board, cook's knife, flat-bladed knife or small spatula, toothpicks, large non-stick ovenproof frying pan, tongs

4 free-range chicken fillets (remove the tenderloin and use for another recipe)

2½ oz/80 g soft goat's cheese

2 tablespoons fresh sage or thyme leaves, finely chopped

3½ oz/100 g roasted almonds or pine nuts, chopped

8 rashers bacon, rind and excess fat trimmed and discarded

1 tablespoon olive oil

2 tablespoons balsamic vinegar

Preheat the oven to 150°C/300°F. Lay the chicken fillets flat on the chopping board. Cut in half right through the middle horizontally so you have two thin flat pieces. Repeat with the other fillets.

Spread the chicken with some of the goat's cheese, sprinkle over the herbs and nuts. Roll up the fillet and wrap bacon around it. Secure with a couple of toothpicks, making sure it is a neat parcel. Repeat with the remaining chicken, filling and bacon.

Heat the oil in a pan over a medium heat. Add the chicken and bacon rolls and cook for 3 minutes each side or until crisp. Drizzle over the balsamic then place the frying pan into the preheated oven and bake, uncovered, for 8 minutes or until cooked through.

NOTE: Don't put too much filling into the centre.

· ·

Fixing What Went Wrong

The fillets were too thick to roll. **Reason:** Fillets were not cut in half. They need to be thin pieces.

The bacon won't stay on. **Reason:** Not secured enough with toothpicks!

A few ingredients and a hot barbecue grill plate is all you need for these delicious chicken pieces!

TANGY LEMON AND DIJON MUSTARD CHICKEN

Serves 4
Cooking style: Barbecue
Other cuts suitable: drumsticks or Maryland (thigh and drumstick joined).

Equipment: chopping board, cook's knife, measuring spoons, fine grater, large mixing bowl, lemon squeezer, tongs, barbecue.

3.5 lb/1.6 kg (size 16) free-range chicken thighs, bone in and skin on (rinsed and patted dry with paper towel)
3 tablespoons olive oil
3 lemons, finely grated rind and juice
2 tablespoons Dijon mustard
salt flakes and freshly ground black pepper

Place the chicken, oil, lemon juice and rind, and mustard in a large mixing bowl and toss well with clean hands to coat the pieces.

Cover with plastic wrap wrap and refrigerate for at least 30 minutes or up to 2 hours.

Preheat the barbecue plate until hot.

Place the chicken on the grill (if your barbecue has a cover, lower it). Cook for 5 minutes without turning. Reduce the heat to medium. Cook a further 8 minutes or until very golden and cooked through, turning often.

Test the chicken by placing the tip of a knife into the thickest section of the thigh—the juices should run clear. If the juices have a pink tinge, place back on the barbecue and cook, covered, for a further 3–5 minutes.

Stand for 5 minutes before serving.

NOTE: For superior crisp skin, begin with rinsing the chicken and patting dry with paper towel.

• •

Fixing What Went Wrong

The chicken was burnt, but undercooked inside. **Reason:** The barbecue is too hot—reduce the heat to medium and turn more often during the cooking.

Simple ingredients, all found in your pantry. You can marinate the chicken in the baking sauce for 30 minutes before baking to add extra flavour!

Serves 4
Cooking style: Bake

Equipment: chopping board, cook's knife, measuring spoons, heavy-based baking dish (cast iron is perfect!), fine sieve

4 scallions/spring onions, ends trimmed, roughly chopped
1 x 15 oz/440 g can good-quality diced tomatoes
1 small red bell pepper/ capsicum, seeds and membrane removed, cut into very thin strips
1 tablespoon balsamic vinegar
1 tablespoon sweet chilli sauce
4 sprigs thyme, leaves removed, stalks discarded
salt flakes and freshly ground black pepper
4 free-range chicken breasts, tenderloin removed (save for another recipe)
3 cups rocket leaves

Preheat the oven to 410°F/210°C.

Arrange the scallions in the baking dish (I use a cast iron heavy dish).

Strain the tomatoes through a fine sieve to remove the excess juice and discard.

Combine the tomatoes, bell pepper, vinegar, chilli sauce and thyme in a medium-sized bowl. Season well with salt and pepper.

Place the chicken fillets in a single layer on top of the scallions. Gently pour the tomato mixture over the chicken.

Bake, uncovered, for 25 minutes or until the chicken is tender and cooked through.

Serve the chicken on a bed of rocket.

NOTE: The peppery rocket is delicious with the balsamic and chilli flavour of the chicken.

BALSAMIC TOMATO ROASTED CHICKEN

· ·

Fixing What Went Wrong

The chicken has stewed. **Reason:** Oven temperature wasn't hot enough.

The sauce has caramelised and burnt. **Reason:** The baking dish was too thin. Use a heavy-based, good-quality baking dish or the sauce will burn easily.

CLASSICS

This classic can be made with thigh fillet, but I like it with large browned pieces of chicken. If you would like to use thigh fillet, please do (see note).

THAI BRAISED GREEN CHICKEN

Serves 4
Cooking style: Simmer/poach
Other suitable cuts: thigh or breast fillet (but be sure to reduce cooking time a little)

Equipment needed:
chopping board, cook's knife, large deep wok or pan, wooden spoon or silicon spatula, can opener, fine grater, lemon juicer, ladle or deep serving spoon

1 tablespoon oil (coconut, sunflower or peanut)
1 x size 16 (3 lb 5 oz/1.6 kg) free-range chicken, quartered
1 large onion, chopped
2 in/4 cm fresh ginger, peeled and finely chopped (or grated)
1 tablespoon Thai green curry paste
14 fl oz/400 ml coconut milk
9 fl oz/250 ml chicken stock
2 Kaffir lime leaves, torn
3½ oz/100 g green beans, cut into 3 cm lengths
1 large carrot, peeled, cut into thin strips
1 tablespoon fish sauce
1 tablespoon grated palm sugar or brown sugar
1 lime, finely grated rind and juice
½ bunch cilantro/coriander, well washed, leaves picked

Heat the oil in the pan over a medium–low heat. Add the chicken pieces and brown well on all sides. Remove from the pan and set aside.

Add the onion, ginger and curry paste and cook, stirring, for 4 minutes or until very fragrant (take care to cook gently).

Stir in the coconut milk, stock and lime leaves. Stirring, bring to the boil then reduce the heat and simmer, uncovered, over a low heat for 5 minutes.

Add the chicken and simmer (do not boil), for about 30 minutes. Add the beans and carrots and cook for 4 minutes or until the chicken is cooked and the vegetables are just tender. Add the fish sauce, palm sugar, lime rind and juice. Taste and add extra fish sauce if needed.

Spoon into serving bowls, top with cilantro and serve with steamed jasmine rice. Garnish with cilantro leaves.

NOTE: Palm sugar and Thai curry pastes are available from Asian food stores or the Asian section of supermarkets.

If you would like to use thigh fillet in place of the large pieces of chicken, add 3 lb 5 oz/1.5 kg thigh fillet, diced to the coconut milk and simmer gently for 8 minutes.

Fixing What Went Wrong

Lack of flavour. **Reason:** The flavour wasn't balanced properly. Thai food is a balance of salty, sweet, sour and heat. Be sure to use good curry paste, fish sauce and palm sugar.

Oily or bitter flavour. **Reason:** The heat was too high. This curry is to be cooked gently—simmer it only!

Lack of colour. **Reason:** Over-cooking the vegetables will destroy their colour and texture—they should be just tender and bright.

An Indian favourite, so I had to include it.

BUTTER CHICKEN

Serves 4
Cooking style: Braise
Other cuts suitable: drumsticks

Equipment: chopping board, cook's knife, measuring spoons and cups, large glass mixing bowl, metal spoon, large heavy-based non-stick frying pan, wooden spoon or silicon spatula

24 oz/750 g free-range chicken thigh fillet, cut in half
2 teaspoons ground cumin
2 teaspoons ground coriander
1 teaspoon ground cinnamon
2 teaspoons garam masala (Indian spice blend)
1 teaspoon turmeric
1 teaspoon paprika
½ teaspoon chilli powder
1 tablespoon vegetable oil (sunflower or peanut)
2 oz/60 g butter
1 onion, finely chopped
2 in/5 cm ginger, peeled and grated
2 cloves garlic, very finely chopped
2 tablespoons lemon juice
5 fl oz/150 ml tomato passata (puree)

3½ fl oz/100 ml chicken stock
7 fl oz/200 ml thickened cream
1 tablespoon honey
5 oz/150 g unsalted roasted cashews, finely chopped

Place the chicken and all of the spices into a glass mixing bowl, stir well to coat evenly. Cover tightly with two layers of plastic wrap and refrigerate overnight. This marinating time is very important, the chicken will hold the flavour of the spices.

Heat the oil in the frying pan. Add half the butter and when foamy add the onion, ginger and garlic and cook over a low heat for 5 minutes or until softened.

Add the marinated chicken mixture, increase the heat and toss the mixture over the heat for about 7 minutes until it starts to brown. Add the lemon juice, tomato passata and chicken stock. Reduce the heat and simmer for about 6 minutes over a low heat,

stirring occasionally. Stir in the cream, honey and the remaining butter. Simmer for 5 minutes but do not boil.

Scatter with or stir through the cashews. Serve with steamed basmati rice.

NOTE: Cream produces the best texture but you can reduce the fat content and replace with evaporated milk if desired.

Fixing What Went Wrong

The sauce is bitter. **Reason:** The onion mixture has burnt. Cook everything gently—burning will cause bitterness and a harsh flavour.

The sauce has curdled or separated with an oily layer. **Reason:** It has been cooked over a high heat and boiled. Once the cream and remaining butter are added, simmer the chicken gently.

This is the homemade version of the 1970's packet soup mix classic. The rich flavour is delicious and will bring back some good old memories. To make this gluten-free, use rice flour.

DRIED APRICOT CHICKEN

Serves 4
Cooking style: Braise

Equipment: chopping board, cook's knife, scissors, food processor, large mixing bowl, tongs, large heavy-based braising or casserole pot with a lid (preferably cast iron or enamel), measuring jug, large spoon or spatula, large plate, paper towel

3 lb 5 oz/1.5 kg free-range chicken drumsticks
salt flakes and freshly ground black pepper
3 tablespoons olive oil
2 large onions, peeled, chopped
2 cloves garlic, peeled, chopped
1 stick celery, strings removed, very roughly chopped
2 tablespoons rice flour or all-purpose/plain flour
2 tablespoons brandy
4 fl oz/125 ml white wine
9 fl oz/250 ml chicken stock
14 fl oz/400 ml apricot nectar
3½ oz/100 g dried apricots, roughly chopped (use naturally dried)

2 teaspoons Dijon mustard

Dry the chicken pieces well with paper towel. Place them into a large bowl. Season well with plenty of salt and pepper and about 2 tablespoons of the oil, tossing well.

Heat the pot over medium heat. Add about half of the chicken pieces and brown well all over (turning often). Remove to a plate. Add the next batch and again brown well until golden and crispy. Remove.

Add the remaining oil and the onion, garlic and celery mixture to the pot. Reduce the heat to low and cook, stirring occasionally for about 8 minutes until lightly golden. Sprinkle in the flour and cook for 2 minutes, stirring. Add the brandy and white wine, stirring well and allow it to evaporate off (it will be bubbly and steamy). Add the stock, apricot nectar, apricots and mustard. Bring to the boil.

Add the chicken pieces and any juices. Stir gently

to cover the chicken in the sauce. Reduce the heat to a simmer and cook, covered, for about 10 minutes or until chicken is tender.

I serve this casserole in the braising dish, straight to the table and make sure there's plenty of mash or rice to soak up all the delicious sauce.

NOTES: If you want, you can remove the skin. Toss the skinless pieces in the oil and season as above. Brown as above, tossing gently in the hot casserole dish.

For a thicker, richer sauce remove the chicken and set aside. Bring the sauce to the boil and simmer uncovered for 6 minutes or until the sauce is reduced and thick. Return the chicken to the pan to serve.

Fixing What Went Wrong

The chicken is pale and flavourless. **Reason:** The chicken wasn't dried well with paper towel and then inadequately browned—this is where all the flavour comes from.

The sauce lacks flavour. **Reason:** Not cooking off the onion-garlic mixture gently. This helps to build the flavour.

Cook this curry slowly so the flavours develop. It's also even better the next day!

CHICKEN AND POTATO CURRY

Serves 4–6
Cooking style: Braise
Other cuts suitable: drumsticks or thigh with the bone in and skin on

Equipment: chopping board, cook's knife, braising pan, deep heavy-based casserole dish or frying pan with a lid, tongs, wooden spoon or spatula

2 lb 4 oz/1 kg free-range chicken thigh fillets, skin removed
2–3 teaspoons korma curry paste
1¾ oz/50 g ghee or 1½ tablespoons vegetable oil
1 large onion, roughly chopped
1 lb/500 g all-purpose potatoes, roughly chopped
2 large carrots, peeled and sliced
1 stick celery, sliced
1 tablespoon all-purpose/ plain flour or rice flour
7 fl oz/200 ml chicken stock
14 fl oz/400 ml good-quality tomato passata (sugo)
salt flakes and freshly ground black pepper, to taste
3½ oz/100 g frozen green peas

Place the chicken pieces and curry paste into a mixing bowl and toss well. Make sure the paste coats the chicken. Set aside.

Heat a pan over medium heat and add the ghee or oil. Add the onion, potato, carrot and celery. Cook for 5 minutes to soften, stirring regularly. Remove from the pan.

Add the chicken pieces to the hot pan and brown well on all sides. Sprinkle over the flour and turn over each piece of chicken. Add the chicken stock, tomato passata, and the vegetables back in. Stir and bring to the boil. Season well with salt and pepper. Partially cover with the lid. Reduce the heat and simmer 30–35 minutes, or until the chicken is tender. Add the peas and cook for 5 minutes.

Serve with steamed rice and pappadams.

NOTES: Ghee is clarified butter and authentic to Indian-style curries.
Be sure the opened jar of curry pastes surface is covered with oil (to keep it fresh), return to the refrigerator and use within 2 months or freeze in small amounts, covered, for up to 4 months.

Be sure to add the peas right at the end to keep the wonderful colour and texture.

Fixing What Went Wrong

The sauce was oily. **Reason:** Too much oil added. After browning the chicken, if the pan looks oily, rub around the base with paper towel.

The sauce is bitter. **Reason:** The onion mixture or chicken pieces were burnt. Cook them over a medium temperature, stirring regularly until just softened.

The classic we all need in our weekly repertoire—this one is loved all over the world. The anchovy is a must in this recipe. Don't worry, you won't taste it but it adds a sensational base flavour.

Serves 4
Cooking style: Braise

Equipment: chopping board, cook's knife, paper towel, heavy based large deep frying pan or braising pan with a lid, silicon spatula or wooden spoon, tongs

1 x Size 16 (3 lb 5 oz/1.6 kg) free-range chicken thighs, with the skin on and bone in
2 tablespoons olive oil
1 onion, roughly chopped
1 carrot, peeled, cut into large chunks
1 stick celery, sliced
½ red bell pepper/ capsicum, cut into thick pieces
3 sprigs fresh oregano, torn or 1 teaspoon dried oregano
1 anchovy, finely chopped or 1 rounded teaspoon Worcestershire sauce
17½ fl oz/500 ml (2 cups) good-quality tomato passata (puree)
2 tablespoons orange juice
4 fl oz/125 ml (about ½ cup) red wine
½ cup pitted Kalamata olives

freshly ground salt and black pepper
2 tablespoons fresh chopped parsley

Pat the chicken pieces dry with paper towel.

Rub the chicken all over with some of the oil and set aside.

Heat the pan over a medium heat. Add the remaining oil, onion, carrot and celery. Cook for about 8 minutes or until golden, stirring often (do not burn). Remove the mixture from the pan and set aside.

Add the chicken thighs and brown well all over. Tip any excess oil from the pan (you can even give the pan a quick rub around with paper towel to remove the excess oil). Return the onion mixture to the pan. Add the bell peppers, oregano and anchovy (or Worcestershire sauce). Stir in the tomato passata, orange juice and wine then bring the mixture to the boil.

Reduce the heat to low and simmer, partially covered, over a low heat for 25 minutes or until the chicken is tender but do not boil. Add the olives and season to taste with the salt and pepper. Scatter with the parsley and serve.

CHICKEN CACCIATORE

NOTE: Make sure you add the anchovy or Worcestershire sauce—it makes all the difference to the flavour.

Fixing What Went Wrong

The sauce was oily. **Reason:** The excess oil was not removed from the pan

The flavour was bitter. **Reason:** The onion was burnt. Be sure to cook the onion until softened and golden. If you burn the onion, remove it and start again.

It is always a treat to cut into the middle of a golden parcel to find the delicious buttery and garlicky (if you like) oozy centre. Traditionally made with dried breadcrumbs, this is always a favourite.

CHICKEN KIEV

Serves 4
Cooking style: Deep-fry

Equipment: chopping board, cook's knife, food processor, rolling pin, plastic wrap, toothpicks, plate, 3 x shallow bowls, balloon whisk or fork, tongs, deep pan or small deep fryer, plate, paper towel

4 x large (about 7 oz/200 g) free-range chicken breast fillets, tenderloin and skin removed (use the tenderloin separately in another recipe)
1 cup dried breadcrumbs or gluten-free dried breadcrumbs
2½ fl oz/70 ml milk
½ cup all-purpose/plain flour or gluten-free flour
3 large free-range eggs, at room temperature
vegetable oil, for frying (you'll need about 2 litres)

Butter Filling
1 cup fresh parsley leaves (use curly or flat-leaf)
½ bunch chives, very roughly chopped
2 cloves garlic, finely chopped (optional, if you're not a garlic lover, leave it out)
6½ oz/190 g butter, at room temperature
salt flakes and freshly ground black pepper
1 lemon, finely grated rind

Fixing What Went Wrong

The crumbing came off. **Reason:** The crumbing wasn't allowed to set in the fridge for at least 30 minutes before cooking.

Start with the butter filling. Combine the herbs and garlic in a food processor and chop. Add the butter, salt and pepper and lemon rind and process until well combined. Tear off 4 pieces of plastic wrap in large squares (around 6 x 6 in/15 x 15 cm) each. Divide the butter into 4. Place a quarter of the butter into each plastic square and roll it into cigar-shaped rolls. Roll up in the plastic and refrigerate for about 30 minutes or until firm.

Using a rolling pin, pat out each chicken fillet evenly to about ½ in/1.2 cm thick. Refrigerate until using.

Unwrap the butter from the plastic and place a chilled log onto the centre underneath side of each chicken fillet. Fold in the edges of each fillet to encase the butter and gently fold it up. Secure the sides with a couple of toothpicks.

Put the breadcrumbs into a bowl and the flour in another bowl.

Whisk the eggs and milk together with the small whisk in another bowl. You will now have 3 separate bowls with mixtures: flour, egg mixture and breadcrumbs.

Lightly coat each stuffed breast fillet in the flour, shaking off the excess. Then coat in the egg mixture and finally in the breadcrumbs, lightly pressing the crumbs on with your fingertips. Repeat with the remaining chicken. Place the crumbed chicken onto a clean plate and refrigerate for 30 minutes.

Heat the oil in a large deep frying pan. Use a thermometer to heat to 350°F/180°C (or add a few breadcrumbs to the oil and they will sizzle and colour within about 5 seconds).

Add the crumbed chicken to the hot oil. Don't over-crowd the pan—if there is not enough room, cook the chicken in batches. Fry for about 3 minutes, gently turning the chicken over in the oil. Cook for another 3–4 minutes or until deep golden in colour. Remove to the plate lined with paper towel and drain well. Remove the toothpicks to serve.

NOTE: Be sure to chill the butter in a log before you place it into the chicken.

The crumbing was golden and crisp but the chicken was not cooked through. **Reason:** The oil was too hot.

The fillet came open and the filling seeped out. **Reason:** The chicken was not secured with toothpicks. Be sure to also evenly flour, egg and crumb the joins.

This is so very delicious. Don't worry about this amount of garlic if you haven't had it cooked like this before—the garlic becomes divinely sweet. Serve with some bread to mop up all those fragrant juices.

CHICKEN WITH 40 GARLIC CLOVES

Serves 4
Cooking style: Braise

Equipment: chopping board, paper towel, kitchen string, scissors, heavy-based large braising dish or pot with a lid, tongs, cook's knife, foil, ladle

1 x size 16 (3 lb 5 oz/1.6 kg) whole free-range chicken
1 lemon, quartered
few sprigs lemon thyme
handful parsley
3 tablespoons olive oil
salt flakes and fresh ground black pepper
5 heads of good-quality garlic
4 fl oz/125 ml dry white wine
10½ fl oz/300 ml chicken stock
1¾ fl oz/50 ml cream (optional)
2 large carrots, peeled and roughly chopped

Preheat the oven to 400°F/200°C (350°F/180°C fan-forced).

Wash and pat dry the chicken well with paper towel. Pop the lemon quarters and herbs into the cavity. Tie the legs together with the string and tuck the wings in (or trim them off).

With clean hands, rub about a tablespoon of the oil over the chicken and season very well with the salt and pepper. Heat a heavy-based large braising dish or ovenproof pot with a lid over a medium heat and swirl the remaining oil over the base. Add the chicken to the pan and brown, turning gently until it is golden all over.

Meanwhile, place the garlic on a chopping board and pull apart all the individual cloves, discard the woody end bit. Do not remove the skin from the garlic.

Add the wine to the pan and allow to bubble away and evaporate. Add the stock and reduce the heat.

Poke the garlic cloves and carrots in the juices around the chicken. Cover with a lid and place into the oven. Bake for about 30 minutes.

Remove from the oven and check the chicken is cooked (using the tip of a knife, test the thickest part of the thigh—the juices should run clear). Remove the chicken to a platter and lightly cover with foil to rest.

Place the pan with all the sauce and garlic over a medium heat and add the cream. Bring to the boil and cook, uncovered, for about 5 minutes or until the sauce thickens to a pouring consistency.

To serve, place the chicken on a large platter, ladle over the softened garlic and carrots and sauce.

NOTES: Choose a heavy-based pan with high sides and a heavy lid. The best size is a pan the chicken and garlic will fit snuggly into.

Be sure to provide small bowls for the discarded garlic skins. To eat the garlic, place the softened clove into your mouth and squeeze out the delicious inside.

- -

Fixing What Went Wrong

The garlic is hard or bitter. **Reason:** Not cooked enough or cooked over a high heat so it burns and becomes bitter (it should be soft and sweet and even slightly caramelised).

The chicken skin has all fallen off. **Reason:** Being too rough when browning the chicken. Turn carefully and don't split the skin.

This will make one large double pastry pie or six individual pies. I like to make my own pastry, it's always a better result (see Hot water Pastry recipe p. 100).

GOOD OLD CHICKEN PIE

Serves 6
Cooking style: Baked

Equipment: chopping board, cook's knife, measuring cups and spoons, food processor, large deep non-stick frying pan or braising pan, rolling pin, knife, pastry brush, small bowl, fork, large metal pie tin

1½ tablespoons olive oil
1 lb/500 g chicken thigh fillets, skin removed, cut into bite-sized pieces
1 large onion, peeled, thinly sliced
3 medium carrots, peeled, ends trimmed, thinly sliced
2 cloves garlic, peeled, thinly sliced
1½ oz/40 g butter
1/3 cup rice flour or all-purpose/plain flour
1¾ fl oz/50 ml white wine
2 cups chicken stock
½ cup milk
1¾ oz/50 g string or long beans, thinly sliced or 1 cup frozen peas
1 quantity of Hot Water Shortcrust Pastry (see recipe p. 100) or 3 sheets of frozen good-quality butter shortcrust,

defrosted
1 egg, mixed with 2 tablespoons milk
salt, for seasoning

Preheat the oven to 350°F/180°C (320°F/160°C fan-forced). Grease the base and sides of an 8 in/22 cm metal pie plate or shallow cake pan.

Heat the oil in the pan over medium heat. Add the chicken, vegetables and garlic and cook, tossing well, for about 8 minutes or until the chicken is cooked and the vegetables are tender.

Stir in the butter. Sprinkle over the flour and stir into the mixture. Cook for 2 minutes, stirring regularly. Add the white wine then the stock and milk. Cook stirring until the mixture bubbles and thickens. Add the beans and stir through. Remove from the heat, set aside and allow to cool completely (see Tips).

Cut out a large circle from the pastry, big enough to line the base and sides of the tin. If using store-

bought pastry you may need to press two sheets together for the circle to be large enough. Lay the pastry inside the tin gently. Place in the filling and smooth the top. Lay some pieces of pastry over the filing and seal and crimp the sides together firmly with your fingertips.

If desired, decorate the top with pastry shapes made from the off cuts. Brush with the egg wash and sprinkle with salt.

Bake for about 40–45 minutes or until the pastry is golden and crisp.

NOTES: Baking in a metal pan means you don't need to blind bake the pastry—it will be golden and lightly crisp.

Always add a cooled or refrigerated mixture to a pie, not hot.

Fixing What Went Wrong

The filling is too thin and oozy. **Reason:** Flour or liquid has been incorrectly measured. The filling must also be brought to the boil and simmered until thick.

The pastry is raw. **Reason:** The oven temperature may be too low. If it is too low, the pastry will not be golden and crisply baked. Also make sure the filling is cooled before adding to the pastry case.

I love this pastry! It's very old-fashioned but the easiest method and recipe for a great simply crisp golden pastry. Make it and roll it out while still warm. To make it very easily, make it in a food processor.

HOT WATER SHORTCRUST PASTRY

Makes enough for base and sides of a deep 9 in/22 cm pie (or 6 medium-sized individual metal tins)

Equipment: scales, measuring cups and spoons, food processor or large bowl, wooden spoon and a flat-bladed knife, medium-sized saucepan, rolling pin, baking paper, clean tea towels, metal tin/tins for baking

10½ oz/300 g unsalted butter
13–14 fl oz/380–400 ml tap water
6 cups (28 oz/800 g) all-purpose/plain flour
1½ teaspoons salt flakes
extra flour, for rolling
1 large egg, mixed with 2 tablespoons milk (optional)

Place the butter and water into a medium-sized saucepan. Bring to the boil.

Place the flour and salt into a food processor and process for 10 seconds. With the motor running, add the hot water mixture in one go through the chute. Process until the mixture forms a soft dough—if the mixture is too soft add an extra ½ cup of flour). The dough will form quickly, so don't over process.

Sprinkle the extra flour on the bench and, using floured hands, bring the dough into a soft ball.

Cut the dough in half. While the dough is still warm, roll out each half between 2 large sheets of baking paper to a large circle until the dough is about ⅛ in/2–3 mm thick. Cover with clean tea towels (to prevent drying out) and allow to rest for 20 minutes.

Roll out to quite thin, about ⅛ in/2–3 mm 2–3 mm (doesn't have to be too thick or it will be heavy and stodgy).

Cut to the desired shape for large pies, small pies, pasties etc. Brush with the egg wash and bake in a hot 400°F/200°C oven.

The pastry does not need to be blind baked for a pie. Always bake in a metal tin and you will have a crisp base and sides.

The pastry is best rolled while warm.

NOTES: Use a food processor and roll while still warm.

To make without a processor: place the flour in a large bowl. Make a well in the centre, with a large spoon. Pour the hot water mixture into the hole. Using a flat-bladed knife, mix and cut the liquid into the flour, mixing to a soft dough.

Fixing What Went Wrong

The pastry is not soft and pliable. **Reason:** Incorrect measuring and chilling of the dough. Roll it out while still warm.

The pastry was crumbly and tough. **Reason:** Over-mixing the dough. Only mix until the dough just comes together.

A family favourite but with a chicken twist! Sear in the flavour by cooking the chicken quickly but take care once you add the sour cream. Perfectly delicious.

CHICKEN STROGANOFF

Serves 4
Cooking style: Pan-fry

Equipment: chopping board, cook's knife, food processor with slicing disk, measuring spoons, scales, large heavy-based frying or braising pan (cast iron is perfect here!), wooden spoon or silicon spatula

3 tablespoons olive oil
1 large onion, peeled, thinly sliced
4 cloves garlic, peeled, thinly sliced
3 free-range chicken thigh fillets, cut into strips
2 tablespoons chicken stock (or dry white wine)
5 oz/150 g button mushrooms (cleaned with a damp paper towel), thinly sliced
1 medium carrot, peeled, thinly sliced
4 sprigs thyme, leaves removed from stalk
3 tablespoons brandy
2 teaspoons Dijon mustard
2 teaspoons Worcestershire sauce
7 oz/200 g natural yoghurt
¼ cup full-cream milk or 9 oz/250 g sour cream
salt flakes and freshly ground black pepper

Heat about 1 tablespoon of the oil in a pan over medium heat. Add the onion and garlic and cook for 3 minutes, stirring until just softened. Remove from the pan.

Add a little extra oil. Reheat the pan to very hot and add half of the chicken, searing it well until golden. Remove from the pan. Repeat with the remaining chicken. Add half of the chicken stock (or white wine) (there will be lots of steam and sizzle) and allow it to evaporate. Remove the chicken from the pan.

Reheat the pan and when hot add the remaining oil, mushrooms, carrots, thyme, brandy and remaining stock, stirring. Cook for 3–4 minutes or until the carrots are just tender and the liquid evaporates. Don't over-cook.

Return the chicken and onion mixture to the pan. Add the mustard and Worcestershire sauce. Toss well and allow to heat through briefly. Turn off the heat and remove the pan from the stovetop. Add the yoghurt and milk or sour cream and gently combine.

Season well with salt and pepper and serve immediately.

NOTE: Don't wash the mushrooms just wipe with damp paper towel.

Fixing What Went Wrong

The result is watery. **Reason:** The chicken has released all its juices. Sear it initially over a high heat to get colour, flavour and seal in the juices and liquid.

The sauce has curdled. **Reason:** You have over-heated the yoghurt and milk or the sour cream. Remove the pan from the heat before adding the dairy and stir through gently.

The flavour and texture of a homemade sausage is just delicious. Vary the herbs to suit your favourite flavour base.

HOMEMADE CHICKEN SAUSAGES

Makes 8 good-sized sausages (recipe can be doubled or tripled)
Cooking style: Poach then pan-fry/barbecue

Equipment: chopping board, cook's knife, stand mixer with food grinding attachment and sausage stuffer, large plate, plastic wrap, large frying pan, char-grill pan (or barbecue), tongs, colander

3 lb 5 oz/1.5 kg free-range chicken thigh fillets, not trimmed
½ bunch flat-leaf parsley, stems trimmed
3 scallions/spring onions, ends trimmed, roughly chopped
2 cloves garlic, peeled (optional)
3 teaspoons salt
freshly ground black pepper
fresh natural sausage casings (well washed), available from a butcher or specialty poultry shop (3.3 feet/1 metre of natural skin makes approx. 5–6 large filled sausages)

Variations
basil and lemon rind
rosemary and black pepper
3 teaspoons curry paste (korma, Thai red etc)
fresh chilli and cilantro/ coriander

Cut the chicken in large thick pieces and lay on a plate, lightly cover with plastic wrap. Freeze for 25 minutes. Meat grinding is best and easier if the meat is partially frozen.

Have all the ingredients ready to use. Attach the food grinder to the stand mixer.

Fit the coarse grinding plate to the food grinder and pop it into the standmixer. Place a bowl under the grinder to collect the minced mixture.

Add the semi-frozen chicken pieces to the food grinder. Mince the chicken, then add all the remaining ingredients into the grinder and mince (working quickly so they all remain well chilled).

Recipe continued.

Fixing What Went Wrong

The mixture is too soft. **Reason:** The chicken is not semi-frozen or not well chilled—keep the chicken very cold.

The skins have split during the cooking. **Reason:** The heat is too high. Poach first gently, then drain and pan-fry or barbecue.

HOMEMADE CHICKEN SAUSAGES

cont.

Fit the flat beater (paddle) onto the standmixer and mix on a low speed (2) for 15 seconds or combine well using a large wooden spoon. The mixture should still be very cold—it should be almost too cold to hold in your hand.

Take handfuls of the mixture and roll into thick log shapes. Place on a clean plate. If the mixture is no longer well chilled, return it to the freezer for 10–15 minutes.

If you do re-chill the mixture, take the time to pull apart the food grinder and wash it well with hot soapy water and dry well. Remember you are working with fresh chicken and must take care to consider and incorporate good hygiene—this is very, very important with raw chicken.

To make the sausages, put the sausage stuffing attachment onto the food grinder then onto the standmixer. Feed the open end of the natural casing onto the stuffer (about 19.5 in/50 cm in length). Leave the other end open.

Turn the mixer to medium low (about speed 4) and start feeding the minced mixture into the grinder. Allow the mixture to slowly fill the skin (don't over-fill or the skin will burst). Keep your speed and pressure even, so the sausages fill evenly.

Lay the large sausage on the clean bench and twist the ends to form links (keep them even in size). Repeat with the remaining skin and minced mixture. Refrigerate until using.

To cook the sausages, I always begin by gently poaching them. This ensures the skins don't split and the texture is soft and succulent as the sausage doesn't burn and dry out.

Place the raw sausages into a large frying pan preferably in a single layer. Cover with cold water. Bring to the boil gently and simmer for 1 minute. Turn off the heat. Drain in a colander. Heat a non-stick frying pan or char-grill over a medium heat. Lightly brush the sausages with oil, then place on the grill or in the pan and cook, turning regularly, until golden brown.

NOTE: You must have fat on the thigh fillets—if the sausages are too lean they will be very dry and not succulent. The poaching removes the excess fat but keeps the texture succulent.

There's nothing better than crumbed chicken and mash, but schnitzel also makes a delicious sandwich filling. Or take some cold pieces along on a picnic or have some sliced, with salad.

Serves 4
Cooking style: Shallow-fry

Equipment: chopping board, sharp knife, rolling pin, hand whisk or fork, 3 wide soup-style bowls, food processor, large deep frying pan, tongs, 2 large plates, paper towel, thermometer

4 x 6 oz/180 g medium-sized chicken breast fillets
4 slices day-old white bread (crusts on or off)
½ cup all-purpose/plain flour (or fine rice flour)
3 large free-range eggs
2 tablespoons water
salt flakes and freshly ground black pepper
24 fl oz/750 ml vegetable oil, for shallow frying

Remove the tenderloin (the long thin piece of chicken underneath) from the fillet.

'Pat out' the chicken fillet with the rolling pin, being careful not to tear it, until it is an even thickness (around 1 in/1.5 to 2 cm).

Place the bread into a food processor and process to fine breadcrumbs (I like to leave the crusts on the bread). Put the crumbs into one of the bowls and the flour into another bowl.

Whisk the eggs and water together in the remaining bowl. You will now have 3 separate bowls, one filled with flour, one with egg mixture and one with breadcrumbs.

Lightly coat each breast fillet in the flour, shaking off the excess. Coat the fillet in the egg mixture and finally coat each fillet in the breadcrumbs, lightly pressing the crumbs on with your fingertips. Repeat with the remaining chicken fillets. Place the crumbed chicken onto a plate and refrigerate for 30 minutes to firm up the crumbing.

Heat the oil in the frying pan until it reaches 350°F/180°C. Use a thermometer to test or add a few breadcrumbs to the oil—they will sizzle and colour within about 5 seconds when the oil is hot enough. Be careful of hot splashing oil.

Add the crumbed chicken to the pan (don't overcrowd the pan—if the pan is too full, cook in two batches). Fry for about 3 minutes or until golden brown. Carefully turn the fillets over, using the tongs, and cook the other side for 3 minutes. Lay on a clean plate lined with paper towel.

NOTES: Always pat out the chicken to even the fillet. When crumbing, use one hand only—keep the other clean, otherwise it gets messy!

The tenderloin can be crumbed and cooked separately but the cooking time should be reduced.

CHICKEN SCHNITZEL

Fixing What Went Wrong

The crumb coating has fallen off. **Reason:** The crumbing is too chunky or too thickly coated. The crumbs should be a fine texture. Make sure you allow the coating time to firm up in the fridge before cooking.

The chicken is raw in sections. **Reason:** The fillet is not even in size and hasn't cooked evenly, or the oil is too hot, or the crumbing has cooked too quickly (a thermometer is the most accurate way to check the oil temperature).

Definitely on the 'last meal' list for me—nothing beats it!

Serves 4
Cooking style: Roast

Equipment: chopping board, cook's knife or scissors, kitchen string, large roasting pan, rack to fit inside the pan, sheet of foil to cover.

1 x size 16 (3 lb 5 oz/1.6 kg) free-range whole chicken
2 lemons, quartered
several sprigs thyme or sprigs of oregano
1¾ fl oz/50 ml olive oil
sea salt flakes and freshly ground black pepper
10½ fl oz/300 ml chicken stock
3½ fl oz/100 ml red wine
1 heaped tablespoon red currant jelly or plum jam

Rinse the chicken well inside and out and pat dry with paper towel.

Preheat the oven to 400°F/200°C. Place a rack inside a large baking dish. It's better to sit the chicken up out of any juices.

Place the lemons and herbs inside the cavity. Tuck the wings underneath (or trim off the bottom section of the wing using scissors, and discard). Tie the legs together firmly with kitchen string.

Use clean hands to rub the chicken all over with olive oil, salt and pepper.

Place the chicken breast-side up into a roasting pan. Add 1¾ fl oz/50 ml water to the pan. This helps to keep the chicken moist and creates wonderful juices in the bottom of the pan for the gravy.

Roast for 1 hour, basting occasionally with some of the oil from the bottom of the pan. Roast a further 30–40 minutes. Test the chicken with the tip of a knife in the thickest section of the thigh. The juices should run clear.

Remove the chicken and set aside to rest, covered lightly with a sheet of foil.

Skim off any excess fat from the roasting pan. Add the stock, red wine and jelly or jam. Bring to the boil, stirring and incorporating all the bits from the bottom of the pan. Simmer for 8 minutes. Taste and add salt and pepper if required.

Serve the chicken and sauce with your favourite roasted vegetables.

NOTE: For amazing crispy skin, pour boiling water over the chicken before cooking. You will see the skin plump up. Pat dry with paper towel before placing in the oven.

CLASSIC ROAST CHICKEN

Fixing What Went Wrong

The chicken was misshapen with the legs cooked apart—looking dry and unevenly cooked. **Reason:** The chicken wasn't trussed properly. For even results always tie the legs together with string and tuck the wings under or remove the tips.

The skin is broken. **Reason:** The skin was torn. Take care not to be rough when turning or moving the chicken.

Soggy underneath and 'water logged'. **Reason:** Always sit the chicken on a rack to roast—the colour and crispness will be even and all over the chicken.

Yes, I love this 'naughty' fried food! When travelling thorough the south of the United States, I always sample it. This is my take on the specialty. It's so worth the frying then baking—the chicken is tender inside and yet gloriously crisp and crunchy on the outside.

SOUTHERN FRIED CHICKEN

Serves 4
Cooking style: Deep-fry

Equipment: chopping board, cook's knife, scales, measuring cups and spoons, large mixing bowl, plastic wrap, large colander, large plastic bag, 3 small bowls, 2 large plates, large deep frying pan or pot, tongs, oven tray or roasting pan, sheet of foil to cover, thermometer

3 lb 5 oz/1.5 kg free range drumsticks or mixed chicken pieces, with the skin on
36 fl oz/1 litre buttermilk (or you can use half buttermilk and half milk)
1½ cups all-purpose/plain flour or fine rice flour
3 teaspoons sweet paprika
2 teaspoons dried oregano
2 teaspoons salt flakes
1 teaspoon cayenne pepper
1 teaspoon ground white pepper
1 teaspoon curry powder (optional, but adds a nice little oomph)
2 large eggs, at room temperature, whisked with 2 fl oz/60 ml water
3 cups fresh breadcrumbs,
processed until very fine (use 1 or 2-day old bread)
17½ fl oz/500 ml oil, for shallow frying

Place the chicken pieces into a large mixing bowl, pour over the buttermilk, cover with plastic wrap and refrigerate. Allow to marinate for 2 hours (or overnight if time permits).

Drain the chicken into a colander, shaking off the excess milk. Place the flour and all the spices into a plastic bag, secure the top and shake to combine. Open and add the chicken pieces, shaking it around to evenly coat.

Remove the chicken from the bag, discarding the flour and bag.

Set up two more bowls and a large clean plate. Add the whisked egg mixture to one bowl and the breadcrumbs to the other.

Dip each piece of the floured chicken into the egg mixture and coat. Drain off the excess then roll in the fresh breadcrumbs, gently pushing the crumbs onto the chicken with your fingertips. Place the chicken onto a plate and repeat dipping and rolling the chicken.

Preheat the oven to 400°F/200°C. Place the rack over the baking tray and set aside until needed.

Fill a large deep saucepan or frying pan with the oil (about 1 in/3 cm). Heat the oil over a medium heat until 375°F/190°C. Use the thermometer to test the temperature or add a few breadcrumbs—they will sizzle if it's hot enough.

Add several pieces of chicken (don't over-crowd the pan) and fry for 5 minutes or until golden. Turn each piece over and brown on the other side. Remove to the roasting tray or pan. Repeat with the remaining chicken.

Cover the pan lightly with the foil and bake for 20 minutes or until cooked through.

NOTE: Be sure to press the crumbs onto the chicken.

Fixing What Went Wrong

The crumbing has fallen off. **Reason:** The chicken was not coated properly in the egg mixture. Also make sure the crumbs are very fine.

The chicken is not cooked through. **Reason:** The chicken wasn't cooked for long enough. Fry then bake—the baking will cook the chicken properly.

MAINS

The meat here is deliciously tender when marinated overnight. I like to use the legs and thigh for this recipe, but you could use any chicken pieces— definitely with the skin on!

BUTTERMILK BARBECUE CHICKEN PIECES

Serves 4
Other suitable cuts: thighs with the bone in and/or drumsticks (skin on)

Equipment: large ceramic or glass baking dish or bowl, tongs and metal spoon, measuring jug and measuring spoons, plastic wrap, barbecue

8 x 5 oz/150 g free- range chicken drumsticks, skin on
10½ fl oz/300 ml buttermilk
1 tablespoon ground fennel
2 teaspoons ground cumin
2 teaspoons ground cinnamon
1 teaspoon ground black pepper
oil, for grill plate
salt flakes, to serve

Place the chicken in the dish. Pour in the buttermilk and spices and swish the whole lot together. Cover with plastic wrap and refrigerate overnight (or for at least 4 hours).

Preheat the barbecue hotplate and lightly oil it. Drain the chicken well and place on a barbecue plate. Cook for 5 minutes before turning to allow the skin to sear and seal.

Turn over the pieces and cook for another 10 minutes or until cooked (if your barbecue has a hood, lower this during the cooking). Test the chicken with the tip of a knife into the thickest section of the thigh. The juices should run clear.

NOTE: Marinate overnight if possible. This will make the chicken so tender.

• •

Fixing What Went Wrong

The chicken is pale and not golden. **Reason:** The barbecue was not hot enough.

The chicken skin has stuck to the grill. **Reason:** You forgot to oil the grill and/or it was not hot enough when you put the chicken on. You also need to make sure you leave it long enough to seal and sear before trying to turn it.

*Chermoula is a delicious punchy paste made with a base of cilantro, lemon, cumin
and a selection of spices, often chilli.*

Serves 4
Cooking style: Braise

Equipment: chopping
board, cook's knife, food
processor, large mixing
bowl, large heavy-based
frying pan with a lid, tongs,
paper towels

4 large free-range chicken
  breast fillets (tenderloins
  removed and saved for
  another recipe)
salt flakes and freshly
  ground black pepper
4 tablespoons olive oil
1 teaspoon ground
  paprika
4 fl oz/125 ml chicken
  stock

Chermoula
½ preserved lemon
3 cloves garlic, peeled
¼ small bunch flat-leaf
  parsley, roughly chopped
½ bunch cilantro/
  coriander, stems
  discarded, well washed
good pinch saffron,
  soaked in 3 teaspoons
  water
½ teaspoon ground
  paprika
½ teaspoon cayenne
  pepper
1 teaspoon ground cumin

1½ tablespoons lemon
  juice
3 tablespoons olive oil
lemon wedges, to serve

Pat the chicken dry with
paper towel. Cut each
fillet into about 5 pieces.
Combine the chicken in
the mixing bowl with the
salt and pepper, oil and
paprika. Refrigerate while
preparing the chermoula.

Wash the preserved
lemon under cold running
water, removing and
discarding all the soft pulp.
Place lemon skin into the
processor with the garlic,
parsley, cilantro, saffron,
paprika, cayenne, cumin
and lemon juice. Process
until finely chopped. Add
the olive oil and process to
combine.

Heat the frying pan over
a high heat until hot. Add
half the chicken and stir-fry
until browned. Remove
from the pan. Add the
remaining chicken and
brown, tossing well. Return
all the chicken to the pan.
Pour over the stock, cover
and simmer 5 minutes, or
until the chicken is tender.

Add the chermoula and
toss well. Cook for about 3
minutes or until the chicken
is tender. Serve with the
chermoula and extra
lemon wedges.

CHICKEN AND CHERMOULA

NOTE: Wash the preserved
lemon very well as it can
be very salty from the
preserving solution.

Fixing What Went Wrong

The flavour is bitter. **Reason:** The chermoula has been overcooked and is possibly a little burnt—it only needs to be
warmed through.

The chicken is tough. **Reason:** The chicken has been boiled with the heat too high and/or cooked for too long. A
chicken breast fillet cooks quickly and meat should only be simmered in the stock—never boiled.

This delicate and gently textured dish is a Japanese favourite. You will need dashi powder, which is sold at supermarkets in the Asian food section or specialty Asian food stores.

CHICKEN DONBURI

Serves 4

Cooking style: Poach

Equipment: chopping board, cook's knife, measuring spoons and jug, large mixing bowl, 2 medium saucepans with lids, whisk, small mixing bowl

1 cup long grain rice, well rinsed, until the water runs clear
1 lb/500 g free-range chicken thigh fillets, trimmed and cut into small bite-sized pieces
1½ tablespoons rice wine (sold at specialty stores or good supermarkets)
2 tablespoons soy sauce
1 teaspoon instant dashi stock powder
7 fl oz/200 ml warm water
2 tablespoons white vinegar
1½ tablespoons superfine/caster sugar
6 shiitake mushrooms, sliced (or any mushroom)
4 large free-range eggs, lightly beaten
4 scallions/spring onions, ends discarded, white and green section, diagonally thinly sliced

Put the rice in a medium-sized saucepan. Add enough water to the rice so that it comes up to the first knuckle of your finger (sit the tip of your finger on top of the rice to measure the water). Cover and bring to the boil, once boiled turn off and set aside (don't take off the lid).

Put the chicken, rice wine and half the soy into the mixing bowl and combine. Set aside to marinate.

Put the instant stock, water, remaining soy sauce, vinegar and sugar into the second saucepan. Bring to a gentle boil and stir to dissolve the sugar. Reduce the temperature to low.

Add the marinated chicken (with the liquid) and mushrooms to the saucepan. Simmer over low heat for about 5 minutes or until the chicken is cooked and the mushrooms are tender.

Remove from the heat. Stir in the egg and set aside, covered, to let the egg set (don't put back on the heat, allow to set gently).

Divide the rice between serving bowls. Spoon over the delicate chicken-egg mixture and scatter with the scallions.

NOTE: Dashi stock adds the correct Japanese flavour to this dish, but chicken stock could also be used.

Fixing What Went Wrong

The egg has curdled and is not gently set. **Reason:** The heat was too high and the egg wasn't allowed to set gently. Remove from the heat and allow to set with the lid on.

Crazy as it sounds, this is a flavour combination you have to try.

CHICKEN WITH ORANGE SLICES AND OLIVES

Serves 4
Cooking style: Pan-fry

Equipment: chopping board, plate, cook's knife, large heavy-based frying pan with a lid, tongs, paper towel

4 free-range chicken Maryland (thigh and drumstick, skin on)
2 tablespoons olive oil
sea salt flakes and freshly ground black pepper
2 teaspoons butter
3½ fl oz/100 ml white wine
7 fl oz/200 ml chicken stock
1 orange, juice and rind
few sprigs oregano, chopped
2 oranges, peeled and sliced
1¾ oz/50 g black pitted olives
2 scallions/spring onions, finely chopped

Pat the chicken dry with some paper towel. Rub some of the oil over the chicken with your fingertips and season well with salt and pepper.

Heat the frying pan over a medium-high heat. Add the oil and butter and swirl. When hot and lightly foamy, add the chicken. If the pan is not large enough for all the chicken, brown it in two batches. Brown the chicken until golden on one side then turn over and brown on the other side.

Add the wine to the pan and allow to evaporate. Add the chicken stock, orange rind and juice and oregano. Reduce the heat to low and partially cover with the lid.

Simmer for 15 minutes or until the chicken is cooked through. To test the chicken, pierce the thigh with the tip of a knife; the juices should run clear.

When cooked, remove the chicken and cover to keep warm. Add the orange slices and olives to the pan and increase the heat. Cook for 5 minutes or until the oranges have softened and the sauce has thickened.

Serve the chicken with the sauce spooned over. This is fabulous with mashed potato!

NOTE: Use pitted olives or if not pitted, be sure to warn your guests or family.

. . . .

Fixing What Went Wrong

The sauce is flavourless. **Reason:** The sauce has not reduced or been simmered for long enough.

The sauce is bitter. **Reason:** The oranges were cooked for too long.

Exotic-flavoured Moroccan tagine of delicious chicken meatballs and whole poached eggs. Serve straight from the pan or transfer gently to a tagine to serve.

Serves 4
Cooking style: Braise

Equipment: chopping board, cook's knife, food processor, measuring spoons, scales, non-stick large frying pan with a lid, tagine (if desired), large plate

2 quarters of preserved lemon
21 oz/600 g free-range chicken thigh meat
1 large onion, cut into wedges
2 cloves garlic, peeled
½ small bunch parsley, leaves picked
½ small bunch cilantro/ coriander, leaves picked (about 1 cup leaves)
2 teaspoons ras el hanout (Moroccan spice blend from specialty stores, good supermarkets)
3 tablespoons cornstarch/ cornflour or all-purpose/ plain flour
salt and freshly ground black pepper to taste
1½ tablespoons olive oil
2 x 14 oz/400 g cans diced tomatoes or 14 fl oz/400 ml tomato passata (puree)
2 teaspoons ground cumin

2 teaspoons paprika
¼ teaspoon ground ginger
4 large free range eggs, at room temperature
fresh cilantro/coriander leaves, to serve

Wash the preserved lemon under cold water, removing the soft underneath pith. Dry well with paper towel and roughly chop.

Using a food processor, process the chicken, onion, garlic, herbs and preserved lemon to a coarse mince mixture (don't over-process, leave some texture). Add the ras el hanout, cornflour, and salt and pepper and pulse briefly to combine. Using wet hands, form large bite-sized balls (kofta) and place on the plate.

Heat the frying pan over medium heat and add the oil. Cook the meatballs until brown. Gently shake the pan often to seal and brown meatballs on all sides, being careful not to break them.

Add the tomatoes, cumin, paprika and ginger. Partially cover with a lid and simmer for 8 minutes or until just cooked.

Carefully break in the eggs among the meatballs (making little nests). Simmer, partially covered, until the eggs are just firm.

Scatter with cilantro to serve.

CHICKEN MEATBALL AND EGG TAGINE

NOTES: Use a non-stick frying pan to brown the meatballs, then transfer if desired to a traditional tagine to simmer until cooked before serving straight to the table in the frying pan or tagine.

Tagines are sold at specialty cookware stores, some are for cooking in others are only for serving in.

• •

Fixing What Went Wrong

The meatballs have all broken up. **Reason:** The meatballs weren't browned carefully before the tomato sauce was added.

The eggs are hard and overcooked. **Reason:** Simmer briefly, partially covered, until the eggs are just firm.

Golden crisp skin encases a moist, flavoursome, chorizo-studded filling. Bake with potato and fennel, for a roast with a difference.

SPLIT ROAST CHICKEN WITH CHORIZO AND LEMON RICE STUFFING

Serves 4–6
Cooking style: Roast

Equipment: chopping board, cook's knife, food processor, non-stick frying pan, wooden spoon or silicon spatula, mixing bowl, kitchen string, large baking dish, paper towel

1 large (size 16/1.6 kg) free-range whole chicken
1 chorizo sausage, roughly chopped
6 scallions/spring onions, tips removed and roughly chopped
2 tablespoons parsley leaves
2 teaspoons olive oil
1½ cups basmati rice, cooked and cooled
1 lemon, finely grated rind and juice
2 lb 4 oz/1 kg unpeeled baby new potatoes, whole (if large, halved)
1 large fennel bulb, ends trimmed, thickly sliced
1 extra tablespoon olive oil
salt flakes and freshly ground black pepper

Preheat the oven to 350°F/180°C (350°F/160°C fan-forced).

Wash chicken well and pat the chicken dry, inside and out, with paper towel. Cut down the backbone of the chicken with your knife (or clean kitchen scissors) from the top to the bottom. Open up the chicken and lie flat, skin-side up on the chopping board. Working gently, use your fingertips to separate the chicken skin from the flesh (taking care not to split the skin), all the way into the leg and thigh section, and the breast.

Place the chorizo, scallions and parsley into a processor and process until finely chopped (or chop finely with a knife).

Heat the oil in the frying pan over medium low heat. Add the chorizo mixture. Cook, stirring occasionally, for 5 minutes or until softened. Stir in the rice and lemon juice and rind. Season with salt and pepper.

Using the back of the spoon or your fingers, push the stuffing evenly up under the skin, into the breast and wing section and down into the thigh and drumstick. Take care not to tear the skin. Gently smooth the skin back over the stuffing. Tuck the wings underneath the chicken. Rub the chicken with the extra oil and season well with salt and pepper.

Lay the chicken on the rack, skin-side up, over a baking dish (to collect all the juices). Place the potatoes and fennel around the chicken.

Roast for 40 minutes, turning the vegetables during the cooking. Test the chicken with the tip of a knife into the thickest section of the thigh. The juices should run clear.

Remove and stand for 10 minutes. To crisp the vegetables (if desired), return the baking dish to the oven and cook, uncovered, while the chicken is standing.

NOTE: Be careful not to tear the skin when stuffing. If you do tear it, secure it with a wooden skewer.

Fixing What Went Wrong

The skin isn't crispy. **Reason:** The chicken wasn't washed and patted dry with paper towel before cooking.

The vegetables underneath the chicken were not cooked. **Reason:** The vegetables needed longer in the oven. If the chicken is cooked but the vegetables haven't, remove the chicken carefully from the pan and wrap in foil to keep warm. Cook the vegetables for an extra 10 minutes.

The mascarpone in this recipe gently melts, making a succulent sauce underneath the crispy golden chicken skin.

CRISPY CHICKEN PIECES WITH MASCARPONE AND BACON

Serves 4
Cooking style: Baked

Equipment: chopping board, cook's knife, measuring spoons, small mixing bowl, teaspoon, large heavy-based non-stick frying pan, baking dish, tongs

1 x size 16 (1.6 kg) free-range chicken
1 tablespoon olive oil
4 rashers bacon, excess fat removed, finely chopped
5 oz/150 g mascarpone
1 sprig basil, stalks discarded
4 sprigs lemon thyme, leaves removed, stalks discarded
freshly ground black pepper
1¾ fl oz/50 ml white wine
3½ fl oz/100 ml chicken stock
salt flakes

Preheat the oven to 400°F/200°C.

Rinse and pat dry the chicken with paper towel. Cut the chicken into four, cutting down through the back into two halves, then separate each half into a leg section and a breast wing section. Trim the end tip from the wing and discard.

Gently use your fingertips to separate and lift the skin from the flesh (enter in from a cut on the side of the chicken). Gently pull the chicken skin back over the flesh to completely cover the flesh and stretch the skin a little. Set the chicken aside.

Heat about two teaspoons of the olive oil in the frying pan. Add the bacon and cook for 8 minutes until lightly crisp. Let cool.

Combine the mascarpone, basil, thyme, bacon and black pepper. Divide the mixture in quarters. Gently place a quarter of the filling under the skin of each quarter of the chicken, smoothing the skin back over the filling. Using your fingertips, rub the remaining oil over the chicken skin.

Arrange the chicken, skin-side up, in the baking dish. Gently pour the wine and stock into the pan around the outside edge (not over the chicken). Bake for 45 minutes until crisp, golden brown and tender.

Serve drizzled with the delicious pan juices.

NOTE: Get your butcher to cut up the chicken if you prefer. Use a good-quality smoky bacon or prosciutto.

•••

Fixing What Went Wrong

The filling has all seeped out. **Reason:** The filling was not smoothed under the skin evenly.

The chicken has singed and stuck to the baking dish. **Reason:** Not enough liquid was added to the baking dish.

Walnuts make a delicious crumbing for this easy pan-fry recipe. Greek yoghurt not only quickens the crumbing process, it also tenderises the chicken.

Serves 4
Cooking style: Shallow-fry

Equipment: chopping board, cook's knife, food processor, 3 wide shallow bowls, 2 plates, rolling pin, measuring cups, spoons and scales, large deep non-stick frying pan, egg flip, tongs, paper towel, thermometer (optional)

5 oz/150 g (1 rounded cup) walnuts
5 oz/150 g (4 slices) day-old white bread, roughly torn into large pieces (I prefer sourdough)
4 tablespoons cornstarch/cornflour
9 oz/250 g Greek-style plain yoghurt
4 medium-sized free-range chicken fillets, skin removed (tenderloins removed and saved for another recipe)
17½ fl oz/500 ml vegetable oil (for shallow frying)
1¾ oz/50 g butter
salt flakes and freshly ground black pepper
lemon wedges, to serve

Place the walnuts into the food processor and process until finely chopped. Remove to one of the bowls and set aside. Add the bread to the food processor and process to fine crumbs. Add to the walnuts in the bowl and gently combine with your fingertips.

Place the cornflour in another of the bowls and the yoghurt into the last bowl (you will have three separate bowls of crumbing ingredients).

Using the rolling pin, pat out the chicken fillet to an even thickness of around 1.2 cm. Be careful not to tear or break it.

Coat each fillet in the cornflour, then generously in the yoghurt and then evenly coat in the walnut crumb mixture. Press the coating on with your fingertips. Place the crumbed fillets on a plate and refrigerate for 30 minutes to set the crust.

Heat the oil and the butter in the frying pan over a medium heat to 350°F/180°C. Use a thermometer or add a few breadcrumbs to the oil, they will sizzle and colour within 5 seconds when it is ready.

Place the chicken into the pan. Cook for 3 minutes, carefully turn over and cook a further 3 minutes on the other side. If chicken does not fit into the pan all at once cook in batches. Don't overcrowd the pan.

Remove the chicken and place on the clean plate lined with paper towel. Season well with salt and pepper and squeeze over the lemon juice to serve.

WALNUT CRUSTED CHICKEN

NOTE: If desired cook the tenderloin separately to the fillet. It has a much quicker cooking time so be careful not to overcook.

Fixing What Went Wrong

The crumbing falls off. **Reason:** The chicken hasn't been coated in the crumbing mixture evenly or the crumbing is too chunky.

The crust is burnt but the chicken is uncooked in the centre. **Reason:** The oil is too hot—you must even out the fillets and make sure each piece of chicken is an even size.

This dish is a Middle Eastern flavour treat. The lemon and olives marry so well with the chicken.

Serves 4–6
Cooking style: Braise
Other suitable cuts: a whole chicken, cut into pieces

Equipment: chopping board, cook's knife, measuring spoons and measuring jug, large frying pan with lid, tongs, paper towel, large mixing bowl, large plate

¼ of 1 whole preserved lemon
8 x 5 oz/150 g free-range chicken drumsticks (skin on)
3 tablespoons olive oil
1 large onion, roughly chopped
2 cloves garlic, finely chopped
10½ fl oz/300 ml chicken stock
½ teaspoon ground ginger
1 teaspoon ground cinnamon
2 teaspoons ground cumin
good pinch saffron threads
4 fl oz/125 ml orange juice
2 dried bay leaves, torn
3½ oz/100 g green olives, stones in
3 tablespoons finely chopped cilantro/ coriander
salt flakes and freshly ground black pepper

Wash the preserved lemon under cold running water, discarding the fleshy inside pulp and very finely slice.

Pat the chicken pieces dry with paper towel and divide into 2 batches. Place into a large mixing bowl and toss with the oil, coating the pieces well all over.

Heat a large deep frying pan over a medium-high heat. Add the first batch of chicken to the pan and brown the pieces lightly, turning often. Remove from the pan, reheat and repeat with the remaining chicken pieces. Remove from the pan.

Add the onion, garlic and about 2 tablespoons of the chicken stock to the pan and cook gently, over a low heat for 5 minutes or until softened. Stir occasionally, incorporating the flavoursome bits and pieces from the bottom of the pan.

Add the preserved lemon, spices, saffron, remaining chicken stock, orange juice and bay leaves, stirring well. Return the chicken pieces to the pan. Partially cover the pan with the lid and simmer over a low heat for 30 minutes or until the chicken is just tender. (Test with the tip of a knife—the juices should run clear.)

Add the olives and half of the cilantro and season well with salt and pepper. Arrange the chicken in a deep serving dish, pour over the liquid. Scatter with the remaining cilantro to serve.

This is wonderful served with roasted potatoes and steamed greens.

NOTE: Wash the preserved lemon thoroughly to remove the salty preserving liquid. A little of this ingredient goes a long way so don't overdo it!

BRAISED CHICKEN WITH PRESERVED LEMON AND GREEN OLIVES

• •

Fixing What Went Wrong

The colour is insipid. **Reason:** Lack of browning. Brown the chicken in batches until lightly golden. This not only ensures a rich colour but also a good flavour.

This is a bit of a great 'saviour' meal in my home. When I can't decide what to cook, this always fits the bill.

QUICK SPICED CHICKEN CURRY

Cooking style: Braise
Other suitable cuts: use breast fillet (but reduce the cooking time to prevent dryness)

Equipment: chopping board, plate, cook's knife or a food processor, large non-stick frying pan, tongs, wooden spoon or spatula, measuring jug and spoons, plate

2 tablespoons vegetable oil (sunflower or peanut is my preferred here)
1 lb/500 g free-range thigh fillets, skin removed (I keep them whole, but you can chop them into smaller pieces if you like)
1 clove garlic, peeled
2 in/4 cm fresh ginger, peeled, roughly chopped
1 large onion, peeled
1 stick celery
2 carrots, peeled
3 teaspoons to 2 tablespoons curry powder (see note)
½ teaspoon ground cumin and cinnamon
1 x 15 oz/440 g can diced tomatoes
4 fl oz/125 ml coconut cream or thickened cream
3½ oz/100 g cauliflower, broken into small florets
3½ oz/100 g green beans, ends trimmed

Heat a frying pan over a medium high heat. Add about 1 tablespoon of the oil and swirl. Add the chicken and brown well for about 5 minutes, turning a few times. Remove and set aside on a plate.

Meanwhile, place the garlic, ginger, onion, celery and carrots in a food processor. Process until chopped. Alternatively, finely chop with a knife.

Add the remaining oil to the pan, with the onion mixture, and all the spices. Cook, stirring, over a medium heat for 3–4 minutes or until softened and glossy.

Return the chicken (and any juices) to the pan and add the tomatoes. Simmer for 5 minutes over a low heat. Stir in the cream.

Add the cauliflower and beans, cover with a lid and simmer gently for 5 minutes. Serve with steamed rice.

NOTE: Buy curry powder in small amounts. More exciting varieties and combinations are sold in Asian food stores. I like a Malaysian mixture. Otherwise, all supermarkets sell basic curry powder.

Fixing What Went Wrong

The sauce is bitter. **Reason:** The onion mixture was burnt. Cook over a low heat and allow to soften gently. Make sure you also gently cook off the spices—the flavour will be better.

ROAST CHICKEN WITH A NUTTY GARLIC ORANGE STUFFING

Serves 4
Cooking style: Roasted

Equipment: chopping board, cook's knife, vegetable peeler, food processor, small spoon, kitchen string, scissors, large baking dish with a trivet or rack inside, large sheet foil, wooden spoon or silicon spatula, measuring spoons, measuring jug, scales

1 large size 16 (3 lb 5 oz/1.6 kg) whole free-range chicken
1 tablespoon olive oil

Stuffing
2 sticks celery, roughly chopped
4 scallions/spring onions (green tops discarded), roughly chopped
2 cloves garlic, peeled
1 in/2 cm ginger peeled, roughly chopped
4 slices bacon, roughly chopped
4 slices (about 4 oz/125 g) sourdough or heavy grain bread
2 oz/60 g macadamia nuts
2 oz/60 g almonds, roughly chopped
1 oz/30 g raisins, roughly chopped

1 orange, finely grated rind and juice
1 large egg
salt and pepper, to taste

Red Wine Gravy
7 fl oz/200 ml red wine
10½ fl oz/300 ml chicken stock
2 tablespoons red currant jelly or plum jam
2 tablespoons tomato paste

. . . .

Fixing What Went Wrong

The stuffing has come out of the cavity. **Reason:** The stuffing wasn't firmly pushed inside the chicken cavity. And be sure to secure the legs together.

The gravy is oily. **Reason:** Remember to spoon off the excess oil from the pan juices before making the gravy.

Preheat the oven to 400°F/200°C (350°F/180°C fan-forced).

Place the celery, scallions, garlic and ginger into a food processor and pulse to chop. Add bacon, bread and nuts and process quickly. Add the raisins, orange rind, juice and egg. Process until the mixture comes together. (Don't over-process, a little chunky texture is nice.)

Rinse the chicken well and pat dry inside and out with paper towel. Spoon the stuffing into the cavity. Tuck the wings underneath (or trim off the bottom section of the wing using scissors and discard). Tie the legs together firmly with kitchen string. Rub the chicken all over with oil. Wrap any excess stuffing in a square of foil and twist the ends to secure.

Place the chicken, breast-side up, onto the rack/trivet in the baking dish. Add 1¾ fl oz/50 ml water to the bottom of the pan.

Roast for 1 hour then baste with some of the oil from the bottom of the pan. Add the foil-wrapped stuffing to the pan, tucking it in beside the chicken. Roast for a further 40 minutes. Test the chicken with the tip of a knife into the thickest section of the thigh. The juices should run clear.

Remove the chicken from the pan and rest for 15 minutes while making the gravy.

To make the gravy, skim off any excess oil from the pan. Place the pan over a low heat. Add the red wine, stock, jam and tomato paste and season with salt and pepper. Bring to the boil, then reduce the heat and simmer for 10 minutes. The sauce will reduce and thicken to a light pouring consistency. Taste and add extra salt and pepper if needed.

Slice and serve with the stuffing.

NOTE: Adding the water to the pan helps to keep the chicken moist and creates wonderful juices in the bottom of the pan for the gravy

Nothing beats chicken and crispy potatoes—brown the chicken well and place on the potatoes so all the delicious juices marry in with the potatoes! Completely delicious!

ROAST GARLIC BUTTER CHICKEN ON SMASHED SPICED POTATOES

Serves 4–6
Cooking style: Roast

Equipment: chopping board, cook's knife, fine grater, citrus juicer, 2 small mixing bowls, teaspoon, heavy-based deep-braising or frying pan, medium saucepan, non-stick frying pan, 2 large wooden spoons or egg lifters, large baking dish, paper towel, kitchen string, potato masher

1 x size 16 (3lb 5 oz/1.6 kg) free range chicken
1¾ oz/50 g butter, softened
3 cloves garlic, finely chopped
1 lemon, finely grated rind and juice
salt flakes and freshly ground black pepper
4 tablespoons olive oil
3 lb 5 oz/1.6 kg small whole waxy potatoes, unpeeled
4 whole onions, skin on, cut into 2 in/1.5 cm large slices rounds (with the skin left on)
3 teaspoons ground cumin
2 teaspoons ground fennel

Rinse the chicken under cold water and pat dry with paper towel. Being careful not to tear the skin, use your fingertips to slide up under the breast skin and down into the leg thigh sections, separating the skin from the flesh.

Combine the butter, garlic, lemon rind, salt and pepper in a small bowl. Use a teaspoon and your fingertips to carefully push and smear this butter mixture under the skin. Tuck the wings underneath and tie the legs together with kitchen string. Rub about 1½ tablespoons of the oil all over the chicken with clean hands.

Heat the pan over a medium heat. Carefully place in the chicken breast-side down and brown well. Turn over carefully and brown the other side (don't tear the skin). Remove from the pan and set aside.

Meanwhile, place the potatoes into a medium-sized saucepan and cover with cold water. Bring to the boil and cook for about 15 minutes or until just tender. Drain well. Remove to the chopping board and with a potato masher, squash the potato, splitting the sides a little.

Preheat the oven to 420°F/220°C. Lay the onion slices and potatoes over the base of the baking dish. Sprinkle over the cumin and fennel.

Lay the chicken on top, breast-side up. Roast for 20 minutes, reduce the temperature to 350°F/180°C and cook for 1 hour. Test the chicken with the tip of a knife into the thickest section of the thigh. The juices should run clear. When cooked, remove from the oven, allow to rest.

Return the vegetables to the oven and cook for 10 minutes for extra crispiness.

NOTE: When browning the chicken, turn over with two large wooden spoons or similar—be careful if using tongs as they will tear the skin.

• •

Fixing What Went Wrong

The chicken is dry. **Reason:** The oven was too hot. Reduce the temperature after the initial 20-minute roasting.

The chicken is misshapen and the legs are dry. **Reason:** Make sure you truss the legs together tightly with kitchen string to keep the moisture inside the chicken.

This stew is so very rich and divine. Serve with steamed greens and rice.

VIETNAMESE CARAMEL BRAISED CHICKEN

Cooking style: Braise
Other suitable cuts: use all thighs, with bone in and skin on

Equipment: chopping board, very large cook's knife, cleaver, large mixing bowl, food processor, measuring spoons and measuring jug, very heavy-based casserole dish with a lid (or a clay pot), tongs, wooden spoon

3 lb 5 oz/1.5 kg free-range chicken pieces (thigh, legs, wings), with the skin on
3½ fl oz/100 ml vegetable oil (peanut, soy, sunflower)
4 cloves garlic, peeled
2 in/4 cm fresh ginger, peeled and roughly chopped
1 fresh red small chilli, stem removed (optional)
2 large onions, peeled and roughly chopped
1 teaspoon each salt flakes and freshly ground black pepper
1¾ fl oz/50 ml soy sauce
3 tablespoons white sugar
1¾ fl oz/150 ml water
1 lime, finely grated rind and juice

½ bunch cilantro/ coriander, leaves picked
½ bunch basil, leaves picked

Chop the chicken pieces into smaller pieces, right through the bone with a very large knife or cleaver. Pat pieces with paper towel until very dry. Place the chicken into the mixing bowl with about half of the oil and the salt and pepper. Toss really well to coat the chicken.

Heat the casserole dish over a medium heat, add about one-third of the chicken and brown well all over, turning often. Remove from the pan. Reheat the pan and add the second batch of chicken and brown, then remove, repeat with the remaining chicken.

Place the garlic, ginger, chilli and onions into a food processor and chop. Remove and set aside

Reheat the pan over medium heat, add the remaining oil and the onion mixture and cook, stirring often, for 5 minutes or until the mixture is golden (do not burn!).

Return the chicken (and any juices) to the pot, add the soy sauce. Cover and reduce the heat to low. Simmer for 15 minutes or until the chicken is tender.

Sprinkle over the sugar, increase the temperature to high and cook, turning the chicken for 5 minutes or until the sugar begins to caramelise (don't burn it!). Pour in the water and lime juice and toss. Reduce the temperature to low.

Simmer uncovered for 5 minutes or until the chicken is tender and the sauce has thickened. Toss through the fresh herbs.

Serve with steamed rice.

NOTE: Make sure to brown the chicken pieces well and use a heavy-based casserole dish.

• •

Fixing What Went Wrong

The sauce is bitter. **Reason:** The onion mixture was cooked over too high a heat and burnt.

The sauce is thin. **Reason:** The sauce has not reduced. Partially covering allows the chicken to simmer and become tender and the sauce to slowly evaporate and reduce to a good consistency.

Delicious and quick to do. You can roast in the oven in or a barbecue with a cover or lid.

SPLIT ROASTED CHICKEN WITH FETA, THYME AND GARLIC

Serves 4–6
Cooking style: Roast/Barbecue

Equipment: large heavy-based baking dish, trivet/rack to fit inside baking dish, cook's knife, chopping board, small mixing bowl, teaspoon, measuring cup, scales, fine grater, paper towel

1 x size 16 (3 lb 5 oz/1.6 kg) free-range chicken
5 oz/150 g feta, crumbled
3 cloves garlic, finely chopped
6 sprigs thyme, stalks removed
½ small bunch chives, finely chopped
¼ bunch parsley, stems removed, leaves finely chopped
1 lemon, finely grated rind
1 oz/30 g butter, softened to room temperature
salt flakes and freshly ground black pepper

Preheat the barbecue or oven to 420°F/220°C. Place a trivet or small rack inside a large baking dish. If using a barbecue, place a rack directly onto the grill (this allows the heat to circulate around the rack and baking dish and prevent the bottom of the baking dish burning).

Wash chicken well, pat dry inside and out with paper towel. Cut down the back bone of the chicken with your knife (or clean kitchen scissors) from the top to the bottom. Open up the chicken and lie flat, skin-side up on the chopping board. Working carefully, use your fingertips to separate the chicken skin from the flesh (taking care not to split the skin), all the way into the leg and thigh section and breast.

Combine the feta, garlic, herbs and lemon zest in a small mixing bowl. Using a teaspoon or your fingers, gently push the cheese mixture in evenly under the skin, pushing it right down into the leg sections and over the breast section.

Smooth the mixture over and gently pull the skin back over the mixture, gently stretching it.

Smear the butter over the skin with clean hands and season well with the salt and pepper. Add ½ cup water to the bottom of the baking dish.

Place the chicken onto the rack in the baking dish skin-side up. Place into the barbecue and cover with the lid, or bake in the oven and cook for 30–35 minutes. Remove and stand for 10 minutes before serving.

NOTES: Cut down through the back bone on the underside of the chicken, not through the breast section.

Adding the water to the pan keeps the chicken beautifully moist as it roasts.

Fixing What Went Wrong

The skin stretched back exposing the filling and flesh. **Reason:** The skin must be gently separated from the flesh and pulled back over the filling—this stretches it.

The chicken has scorched and stuck to the baking dish. **Reason:** The chicken wasn't placed on a rack inside the baking dish and/or the baking dish not placed on a rack inside the barbecue.

This easy, tasty recipe was shared with me by my friend Katy. I've tweaked it a little to make it my own but it was a gorgeous starting point. Serve with plenty of steamed basmati or brown rice and green beans.

STICKY BAKED LEMON CHICKEN

Serves 4

Cooking style: Pan-fry and bake

Other suitable cuts: thighs, legs or wings (skin on)

Equipment: heavy-based braising or casserole pot, large plastic bag, measuring cups and spoons, measuring jug, fine grater, tongs

4 x 10½ oz/300 g free-range chicken Maryland (the thigh and leg), bone in, skin on, cut into pieces
½ cup all-purpose/plain flour or rice flour
2 teaspoons ground cumin
2 teaspoons ground sweet paprika
½ teaspoon chilli powder (if you like a touch of heat)
salt flakes and freshly ground black pepper
3 tablespoons coconut oil or any vegetable oil (the coconut oil adds a lovely flavour and colour)
2 lemons, finely grated rind and juice
4 fl oz/125 ml dry white wine
2 tablespoons soy sauce
2 medium green apples, roughly chopped (you could also use pineapple or fresh dates—the touch of sweetness is lovely in this tangy sauce)
4 whole red chillies (optional)

Preheat the oven to 400°F/200°C fan-forced (or 420°F/220°C)

Place the chicken into the plastic bag with the flour, all the spices and plenty of salt and pepper. Seal the bag and shake well to coat the chicken. Remove the chicken and discard the bag.

Heat the oil in the pot over medium heat. Gently pan-fry the chicken, turning it over and browning on all sides. Remove the chicken from the pan and discard all of the oil. Return the chicken to the pan.

Add the lemon rind, juice, wine and soy sauce. Add in the fresh fruit and the whole chilli. Bake, uncovered, for 30 minutes or until the chicken is tender and cooked through.

NOTE: Brown the chicken well over a medium heat for a wonderful colour.

* * *

Fixing What Went Wrong

Chicken was too oily. **Reason:** The excess oil wasn't removed before the chicken was baked.

The skin has fallen off. **Reason:** Over-turning or being too rough during the browning process. Be gentle and only turn a few times, leaving it to get brown in-between.

You can use fettuccine if you like. A quick pasta dish with oomph.

Serves 4
Cooking style: Pan-fry and simmer

Equipment: chopping board, cook's knife, large saucepan with lid, large spoon, tongs, colander, large deep non-stick frying pan, wooden spoon or silicon spatula, fork

1 lb/500 g dried spaghetti
6 slices thin prosciutto
2 tablespoons olive oil
1 tablespoon (²/3 oz/20 g) butter
1 onion, diced
2 cloves garlic, finely chopped
1 red chilli, finely chopped
12 oz/350 g chicken mince
10½ oz/300 g button mushrooms, sliced
4 fl oz/125 ml (½ cup) white wine
7 fl oz/200 ml (¾ cup) tomato passata (or puree)
1 orange, finely grated rind and juice
1 sprig rosemary, leaves removed and chopped
salt flakes and freshly ground black pepper

Cook the pasta in the saucepan of boiling salted water for 8–10 minutes, drain well and return to the saucepan. Cover and keep warm.

Meanwhile, heat a frying pan over medium heat. Add the prosciutto and cook for about 4 minutes or until very crispy. Remove and crumble into large pieces.

Heat the oil and butter in the frying pan, over medium heat. When foamy add the onion, garlic and chilli and cook stirring for 5 minutes or until softened. Add the chicken mince, breaking up any lumps with a fork. Cook for 3 minutes, or until just done. Add the mushrooms and cook, stirring, for 3 minutes.

Stir in the wine and allow to evaporate. Add the tomato passata, orange rind and juice, rosemary and season well with salt and pepper. Simmer for 5 minutes, taste and season with more salt and pepper if needed.

Toss the sauce with the pasta, crumble over the prosciutto and serve.

SPAGHETTI WITH CHICKEN, PROSCIUTTO AND MUSHROOMS

NOTE: You can make your own chicken mince quickly and easily in a food processor or with a food grinder on a standmixer using chicken thigh fillets.

Fixing What Went Wrong

The sauce lacks flavour. **Reason:** The pan wasn't hot enough to sear the onion mixture or mince. The flavour comes from this important cooking step, which also uses the flavour in the pan from the prosciutto.

The chicken in the sauce is dry and tough. **Reason:** The chicken has been overcooked. Chicken mince is lean and toughens easily especially if breast fillet is used for the mince.

STIR-FRIES

Yes, this is the real thing—the favourite we all ordered. I have added a little pork into this but you can add shrimp/prawns if you like.

CHICKEN CHOW MEIN

Serves 4
Cooking style: Stir-fry

Equipment: chopping board, cook's knife, small mixing bowl, measuring spoons, vegetable peeler, very small bowl, wok with a lid, wok charn or large metal spoon, strainer, large mixing bowl

4 dried shiitake mushrooms (I use whole ones for this recipe)
14 oz/400 g free-range chicken thigh fillets, diced
2 tablespoons Chinese rice wine (known as shao xing rice wine) or dry sherry
2 tablespoons soy sauce
¼ in/4 cm fresh ginger, peeled and finely chopped (or grated)
about 2 tablespoons cornflour (or potato flour)
4 tablespoons vegetable oil (peanut or sunflower)
3½ oz/100 g pork loin, cut into strips (or raw shrimp/ prawn meat)
1 bunch baby bok choy, washed, ends trimmed and cut into thick strips lengthwise
½ bunch scallions/spring onions, ends trimmed and discarded, cut into 1 in/2 cm lengths
4 tablespoons (⅓ cup) chicken stock
10½ oz/300 g fresh egg noodles, gently separated with your fingertips (found in refrigerated section of supermarket)
3 teaspoons sesame oil

Place the mushrooms in a mixing bowl and pour over boiling water to cover (poke the mushrooms down into the water). Soak for about 20 minutes or until rehydrated. Drain through the strainer over the large mixing bowl keeping all the mushroom liquid. Cut the mushrooms in half, discard the stalk (it's always tough). Set aside.

Combine the chicken, rice wine, 1 tablespoon soy sauce, ginger and 1 tablespoon of the cornflour in a mixing bowl, mixing well. If time allows, cover and pop into the fridge to marinate for 30 minutes.

Heat the wok to very hot. Add about 1½ tablespoons of the oil and swirl. Add half of the chicken and stir-fry for about 3 minutes or until golden and nearly cooked. Remove from the wok. Reheat and add a little more oil and the remaining chicken. Stir-fry and remove. Add the pork to the wok and toss well, cook for about 1 minute (it will cook very quickly). Remove and set aside with the chicken.

Add the bok choy, scallions and the stock. Toss well, bring to the boil. Add the noodles and gently toss, separating the noodles. Cover with the lid and cook for 2 minutes.

Return all the chicken, pork (and any juices), mushrooms and liquid to the pan and add the sesame oil. Combine the remaining cornflour with the soy sauce and stir into the noodles, tossing well and allow to reheat and thicken. Serve immediately.

NOTE: Be sure to separate the noodles, so they don't clump together.

Fixing What Went Wrong

The mushrooms were hard. **Reason:** Not soaked for long enough. More soaking is needed to rehydrate properly—*discard the tough stalk.*

Flavour was lacking. **Reason:** Marinate the chicken to give the meat time to absorb the flavour and be sure to sear it well. Don't forget the ginger and sesame oil, they are a must.

Bean thread noodles are an interesting textured noodle. They have a firm yet tender bouncy texture. They are very inexpensive and a great handy noodle to have in the pantry.

Serves 4
Cooking style: Stir-fry

Equipment: chopping board, cook's knife, large mixing bowl, colander, wok with a lid, wok churn or large metal spoon, plate, tongs, scissors

7 oz/200 g dried bean thread noodles, string removed and discarded (usually sold in string wrap bundles)
1 lb/500 g free-range skinless chicken thigh fillets, thinly sliced diagonally
3 cloves garlic, finely chopped
3 small red chillies, very finely chopped (or use 1 teaspoon prepared chilli paste)
salt flakes and freshly ground black pepper
4 tablespoons vegetable oil (peanut, soybean, corn or sunflower)
5 oz/150 g whole baby corn
1 bunch scallions/spring onions, end trimmed, cut into 2 in/4 cm lengths
1 teaspoon white sugar
2 tablespoons chicken stock or water

2 tablespoons hoisin sauce
1 tablespoon soy sauce

Place the noodles into a large mixing bowl and cover with warm water. Let soak for 20 minutes or until softened. Drain well into a colander. Using scissors, roughly chop into long lengths. Cover to keep warm.

Meanwhile, combine the chicken, garlic and chilli with a teaspoon of the salt and pepper and mix well.

Heat a wok over a high heat until slightly smoking. Add 1 tablespoon oil and swirl. Add about one-third chicken to the wok and stir-fry for 3 minutes or until just tender. Remove from the wok. Reheat the wok and repeat with the remaining two batches of chicken, set aside.

Add the baby corn and scallions to the hot wok, sprinkle over the sugar and stock or water. Toss well. Cover and allow to steam for 2 minutes or until just tender. Return the chicken and all the juices to the

wok. Add the sauces and toss well.

Divide the noodles between serving bowls. Top with the chicken and vegetables and serve.

NOTE: Start the chicken cooking about two-thirds of the way through the noodles soaking. Don't cook the chicken and have it sitting – it needs to be seared and served immediately.

GARLIC AND CHILLI CHICKEN WITH BEAN THREAD NOODLES

Fixing What Went Wrong

The noodles are tough. **Reason:** Not soaked in water that is warm enough—the bean thread noodles are quite hard if not softened enough.

Too much sauce. **Reason:** Not measuring the liquid ingredients correctly, too much sauce and the stir-fry looks drowned—it should look moist.

The mushrooms and walnuts combine to add a special flavour to this simple stir-fry.

HOKKIEN NOODLE, MUSHROOM AND WALNUT STIR-FRY

Serves 4
Cooking style: Stir-fry

Equipment: chopping board, cook's knife, measuring spoons and cups, large mixing bowl, kettle, colander, large wok or frying pan, wok charn or large metal spoon, tongs

3½ oz/100 g (1 cup) dried sliced shiitake mushrooms
4 tablespoons vegetable oil (peanut, soy bean, corn or sunflower)
1 lb/500 g free range skinless chicken thigh fillets, thinly sliced on the diagonal
14 oz/400 g baby bok choy, ends trimmed and cut in half lengthwise, washed
3½ oz/100 g (1 cup) walnuts or almonds, very roughly chopped
3 tablespoons Chinese rice wine or dry sherry (also known as shao xing rice wine)
14 oz/400 g packet fresh hokkien noodles, gently pulled apart
3 tablespoons oyster sauce
3 tablespoons chicken stock
2 tablespoons soy sauce
2 tablespoons brown sugar
2 teaspoons sesame oil

Place the mushrooms in a large mixing bowl, cover with boiling water and stand for 30 minutes or until the mushrooms are tender. Drain well, discarding the water. Set aside.

Heat the wok until very hot over high heat. Add about half of the oil and swirl quickly. Add about ⅓ of the chicken and toss and stir-fry for 1 minute. Remove from the wok. Reheat the wok, add a little more oil and repeat with the next batches of the chicken.

Add the remaining oil, bok choy and walnuts to the wok and toss well. Cook for about 30 seconds. Add the wine (or sherry) and cover with the lid. Cook for 30 seconds or until the bok choy wilts and softens. Remove from the wok. (Don't over-cook!)

Return all the chicken (and any juices) to the wok, add the noodles, mushrooms, oyster sauce, stock, soy sauce and sugar. Toss for 2 minutes or until warmed through.

Add the bok choy and walnut mixture and sesame oil. Serve immediately

NOTE: Break up the cold noodles with your fingertips (don't add to the wok in a big clump).

Fixing What Went Wrong

The mushrooms are tough. **Reason:** Mushrooms haven't been soaked enough. Soak the mushrooms in hot water to reconstitute and soften.

The stir-fry is soggy and limp. **Reason:** Over-cooking. Cook this recipe in a hot wok. Toss well and quickly. Serve immediately while piping hot.

This is the best stir-fry made in a flash! I purchased frozen chopped lemongrass, found in the freezer section at Asian food stores. But you can also prepare the lemongrass in the food processor.

LEMONGRASS AND CHILLI CHICKEN

Cooking style: Stir-fry

Other suitable cuts: sliced breast fillet (but take care not to over-cook)

Equipment: chopping board, cook's knife, food processor, mixing bowl, large wok with a lid, wok charn or large metal spoon, paper towel

2 lb 4 oz/1 kg free-range chicken breast thigh fillets, patted dry with paper towel and cut into thick strips

2½ fl oz/80 ml vegetable oil (sunflower, peanut or soybean)

salt flakes and white pepper, to taste

3 cloves garlic, chopped

3 tablespoons finely chopped fresh frozen lemongrass, or 3 fresh stalks (see note)

2–4 fresh small red chillies, roughly chopped (as much as you can handle)

2 teaspoons white sugar

2 teaspoons fish sauce or soy sauce (fish sauce gives a Vietnamese touch, soy adds a Chinese touch)

1¾ fl oz/50 ml water

Combine the chicken with about half of the oil and plenty of the salt and pepper and mix well to coat the chicken.

Heat the wok over a high heat until very hot, add a tablespoon of the oil and swirl. Quickly add the garlic, lemongrass and chilli and toss a couple of times (don't burn this). Remove from the wok.

Add about half of the chicken and stir-fry, tossing well to brown. Cook for about 3 minutes, remove from the wok. Reheat the wok, adding the remaining oil and chicken. Cook for about 3 minutes.

Return all the chicken and lemongrass mixture to the pan, sprinkle over the sugar and toss well. Add the fish sauce or soy sauce and water. Cover and steam for 2 minutes or until the chicken is cooked.

NOTE: To prepare the lemongrass, trim the very bottom of the stem and the green section and discard. Peel off the hard outside leaves and discard. Roughly chop the tender inside section into 2 in/4 cm lengths. Place into a food processor and process until finely chopped.

Fixing What Went Wrong

The stir-fry has lots of liquid and is water-logged. **Reason:** The wok was not hot enough and the chicken has stewed.

The lemongrass is tough and stringy throughout the stir-fry. **Reason:** You have used the outside tough leaves. Always discard these and use only the tender insides. Or purchase ready-chopped and frozen lemongrass, it's sensational and very cheap to buy.

A Chinese flavour base inspires this 15-minute quick stir-fry. Pop the rice on first and you will have a delicious meal in minutes.

MINCED CHICKEN WITH FRESH HERBS AND BROCCOLI

Serves 4
Cooking style: Stir–fry
Other suitable cuts:
minced chicken breast or thigh fillet

Equipment: chopping board, cook's knife, vegetable peeler, food processor, large wok, wok charn or large metal spoon, measuring spoons

1 cup (1¾ oz/50 g) fresh herbs such as cilantro/ coriander, basil, mint leaves
1 lb/500 g free-range chicken breast fillet, skin removed, well chilled, roughly chopped into large pieces
4 scallions/spring onions, green tips discarded, very roughly chopped
4 cloves garlic, peeled
2 in/4 cm fresh ginger, peeled and roughly chopped
2 carrots, peeled
3 tablespoons coconut oil or vegetable oil
good pinch salt flakes
1 head broccoli, broken into florets
2 tablespoons rice wine or sherry
1 tablespoon soy sauce

1 tablespoon coconut rice vinegar or rice wine vinegar
several drops sesame oil
steamed rice, to serve

Put the herbs into the food processor and chop then remove from the bowl. Add the chicken and process until chopped but still with a little texture. Remove and set aside.

Wash and dry the bowl, chopping blade and the processor cover.

Place the scallions, garlic and ginger into the clean bowl and chop. Remove.

Attach the slicing disc to the processor. Thinly slice the carrots, remove and set aside.

Heat the wok over a high heat, add the coconut oil and swirl. When slightly smoky add the chicken mince and salt. Stir-fry, breaking up all the lumps. Cook for about 3 minutes. Remove and set aside.

Add the vegetables to the wok and toss. Add the

rice wine and cook until evaporated. Add the soy sauce and vinegar and cook for 30 seconds.

Return the chicken mince to the wok with the sesame oil and fresh herbs and toss well to warm through.

Serve immediately with the steamed rice.

NOTE: Use the food processor to mince your own chicken—you'll have the freshest possible mince without any additives. The processor is also great for the garlic and ginger and carrots.

You can do all your chopping by hand, if preferred, and use pre-made mince.

Fixing What Went Wrong

The mixture was watery. **Reason:** The wok was not hot enough. The wok must be slightly smoking and the chicken is seared very quickly.

The freshness is lost. **Reason:** Don't overcook! This is a 'have everything ready and toss in the wok and eat' recipe!

Use thigh fillet for this stir-fry—the texture and flavour is so much better.

Serves 4
Cooking style: Stir-fry

Equipment: chopping board, cook's knife, peeler, fine grater, large wok with a lid, wok charn or large metal spoon

2 tablespoons vegetable oil (peanut, soybean or sunflower)
10½ oz/300 g chicken thigh fillet, cut into thin long pieces
2 in/5 cm ginger, peeled and finely grated
2 cloves garlic, chopped
good pinch white sugar
good pinch salt
3½ oz/100 g cauliflower, broken into small florets (little pieces)
2 tablespoons chicken stock or water
3½ oz/100 g snow peas, strings removed
2 teaspoons sesame oil
extra salt and black pepper, to season
handful of fresh bean sprouts, to serve
chopped chives, to serve

Heat a large wok over a high heat until lightly smoking. Add the oil, chicken, ginger, garlic, sugar and salt. Toss over a high heat for 3 minutes or until golden brown.

Add the cauliflower and stock and toss well. Cover with a lid and cook for 1 minute. Add the snow peas and toss then cover and cook for a further 1 minute or until the snow peas are just tender.

Sprinkle over the sesame oil and season with extra salt and pepper. Serve topped with the fresh sprouts and chives.

QUICK GINGER CHICKEN, SNOW PEA AND CAULIFLOWER TOSS

NOTE: Choose a large flat-bottomed wok and always heat until lightly smoking.

. . . .

Fixing What Went Wrong

The stir-fry is watery. **Reason:** The wok was not smoking hot.

The cauliflower is tough. **Reason:** The cauliflower was stir-fried, but not steamed. You need to cover and steam the vegetables a little.

Delicious tender wafer-thin pieces of chicken, tossed with ribbons of zucchini, carrot and lashings of ginger and garlic. The quickest way to cut everything is to pop it through the thin slicing blade on your food processor.

CHICKEN WITH ZUCCHINI AND CARROT RIBBONS

Serves 4
Cooking style: Stir-fry

Equipment: chopping board, cook's knife, scissors, vegetable peeler, measuring spoons, food processor with thin slicing blade, large wok with a lid, or large frying pan, wok charn or large metal spoon, tongs

2 large free-range skinless chicken breasts, partially frozen
3 large carrots, peeled
2 medium zucchini, ends trimmed
sea salt and freshly ground black pepper to taste
1 tablespoon vegetable oil (peanut, soybean, sun flower)
2 cloves garlic, crushed
2 in/5 cm ginger, finely grated
1 teaspoon ground fennel or finely grated rind of 1 lemon
3½ oz/100 g fresh rice noodles, snipped into 4 in/8 cm lengths (use a sharp knife or scissors)
2 tablespoons chicken stock or water
soy sauce, to taste

Using a food processor with a thin slicing blade, thinly slice the chicken (making sure it's partially frozen for easy cutting). Remove and set aside.

Wash and dry the bowl then thinly slice the carrot and zucchini (you can also use a sharp knife for the chicken and a vegetable peeler for the veggies).

Heat a wok or a pan over a medium heat until really hot. Add the oil, garlic, ginger and chicken with plenty of salt and pepper. Toss very well. When starting to cook on the edges (about / 2 minutes) add the carrot and zucchini and keep tossing. Cook for about 30 seconds.

Add the fennel or lemon rind, fresh rice noodles and water and cook, breaking up the noodles if they are firm. Cover with a lid and cook for 30 seconds or until noodles have softened. Toss well. Season with soy sauce and serve immediately.

NOTE: Asian food stores sell fresh rice noodles in the refrigerator section. They only require reheating until softened. You can buy flat blocks that need slicing or cute 'ribbons'. If not available, sticks of dried rice noodles may also be used. Dried noodles will need soaking or quickly cooking in boiling water before being added.

Fixing What Went Wrong

The chicken stewed. **Reason:** The temperature in the wok dropped. It must be smoking hot.

The chicken is tough. **Reason:** You have over-cooked it. Breast fillet needs the quickest cooking in a stir-fry. Thigh fillet can also be used and tends to not toughen.

The zucchini is bitter. **Reason:** Old zucchini can be bitter, choose fresh young vegetables that have firm and smooth, quite shiny looking skin.

Always a favourite! Have everything prepared and measured out before cooking. Don't forget the fish sauce, chilli, lime and chopped peanuts to serve.

Serves 4
Cooking style: Stir-fry

Equipment: chopping board, cook's knife, large mixing bowl, small mixing bowl, balloon whisk or fork, colander, wok, tongs

9 oz/250 g dried rice stick noodles

6 tablespoons vegetable oil (or peanut, soy, sunflower)

1 lb/500 g chicken thigh fillets, cut into small dice

3 Asian shallots, peeled and finely sliced (sold in Asian food stores or use scallions/spring onions)

2 cloves garlic, chopped

2 small red chillies, finely chopped (discard the seeds for a milder flavour)

2 limes, finely grated rind and juice

2½ fl oz/75 ml fish sauce

1 oz/30 g palm sugar, finely grated or chopped (sold at supermarkets and Asian food stores)

2 large eggs, well beaten

½ bunch cilantro/coriander, washed, dried and chopped

4 oz/125 g bean sprouts

½ bunch garlic chives, chopped

3½ oz/100 g peanuts, roasted and chopped

½ bunch garlic chives, chopped, to serve

3½ oz/100 g roasted chopped peanuts, to serve

1 lime, cut into wedges

2 chillies, very finely sliced

4 oz/125 g bean sprouts

Place the rice stick noodles into a large mixing bowl, cover the noodles with very warm water (from the tap). Stand for about 8–9 minutes or until just softened. Drain well into the colander. Set aside.

Heat a wok over a high heat until very hot. Add 2 tablespoons oil and heat, swirling around the wok to coat. Add about one-third each of the chicken, shallots and garlic, tossing well. Stir-fry for 3 minutes or until the chicken is golden. Remove from the wok. Repeat with two more batches of oil, chicken, shallots and garlic, making sure you reheat the wok well in between each batch.

Return all the chicken mix to the wok, add the drained noodles, chilli, lime rind and juice, fish sauce and palm sugar. Toss well. Add the eggs and toss very well then turn down the heat (the egg needs to coat the noodles and just warm through). Add the cilantro, bean sprouts, chives and peanuts. Toss well. Take care not to overcook.

Serve in bowls with the extra ingredients on the side.

PAD THAI CHICKEN

NOTE: Add 3½ oz/100 g raw shrimp/prawn meat to the last batch of chicken if desired.

Fixing What Went Wrong

The noodles are broken up and soggy. **Reason:** The water was too hot and/or the noodles were soaked for too long.

The egg has burnt or curdled over the noodles. **Reason:** The noodles were cooked for too much longer after the eggs have been added.

I love the spicy oomph to Cambodian food. This is cooked in a pan, not a wok and is a little gentler than a Chinese-style stir-fry.

Serves 4
Cooking style: Stir-fry

Equipment: chopping board, cook's knife, food processor, measuring spoons, measuring jug, large deep frying pan, wooden spoon or large metal spoon

2 tablespoons vegetable oil (peanut, corn or sunflower)
2 large onions, peeled, chopped
3 cloves garlic, finely chopped
2 large free-range chicken fillets, cut into small pieces
2 stalks lemongrass, outside leaves and green section discarded, very finely chopped
3 small red chillies (seeds discarded for a milder flavour), finely chopped
2 teaspoons ground turmeric
9 fl oz/250 ml (1 cup) good chicken stock
1½ tablespoons soy sauce
1 tablespoon fish sauce
2 teaspoons sugar
1 cup fresh basil leaves, roughly torn

Heat the oil in the frying pan over a medium heat. Cook the onions and garlic for 4 minutes or until lightly golden. Add the chicken and stir well, combining with the onions. Toss well and cook, stirring often for 3 minutes or until golden.

Add the lemongrass, chilli and turmeric. Stir to combine. Add the stock, soy sauce, fish sauce and sugar. Simmer gently, stirring occasionally, for about 7 minutes or until the chicken is tender. Stir in the basil. Serve immediately.

SPICY CAMBODIAN CHICKEN STIR-FRY

NOTE: Cook the onion and garlic separately before adding the chicken. The other aromatic ingredients (lemongrass and chilli) are added after this.

Fixing What Went Wrong

The chicken is tough. **Reason:** Cooked too fast. Stir-fry lightly then simmer in the stock gently.

The flavour balance is too salty. **Reason:** Too much fish sauce or no sugar. Measure the ingredients for a perfect balance between sweet and salty.

These noodles are sold fresh in all Asian food stores. The texture is delicious—soft and a little slippery.

THICK RICE NOODLES WITH SEARED SOY CHICKEN

Serves 4
Cooking style: Stir-fry

Equipment: chopping board, cook's knife, measuring spoons, large mixing bowl, medium mixing bowl, small bowls, teaspoon, colander, tongs, large wok, wok charn or large wooden spoon, measuring cups

1 lb/500 g fresh rice noodles (sold in blocks at Asian food stores)
1 large free-range chicken fillet, skin removed
2 in/5 cm fresh ginger, peeled
3 scallions/spring onions, ends trimmed and discarded
1 cup bean sprouts
3 tablespoons vegetable oil (peanut oil is great for this recipe)
2 teaspoons soy sauce
1½ teaspoons cornstarch/ cornflour, mixed to a paste with 1 tablespoon cold water
salt flakes and ground white pepper
2 teaspoons light soy sauce

Using a sharp knife, cut through the noodles into strips. Place in a large mixing bowl. Pour over hot water and allow to stand for 10 minutes, gently separating the noodles (take care to separate and not tear).

Meanwhile, diagonally slice the chicken (have it very chilled or even half frozen) into very, very thin slices. Place into a medium mixing bowl. Very, very thinly slice the ginger and finely chop the scallions.

Drain the noodles into a colander and set aside.

Add about 1½ tablespoons of the oil to the chicken with a little of the soy sauce and about 2 teaspoons of the cornflour paste and the salt and pepper. Mix well.

In a large wok, add the remaining oil and heat until smoking hot, swirl to coat. Add the chicken and ginger and toss well, stir-fry until lightly golden (about 2 minutes only). Add the bean sprouts and scallions and toss for about 15 seconds. Remove from the wok and set aside.

Add the noodles, remaining soy sauce and the cornflour mix. Toss well. Return the chicken and vegetables to the wok and toss. Serve immediately.

NOTE: Have all the ingredients ready before you start to cook.

Fixing What Went Wrong

The rice noodles have disintegrated. **Reason:** They were heated with boiling water. They only need warming through. Be gentle when separating.

The noodles have all stuck to the bottom of the wok. **Reason:** Not enough stirring. This stir-fry is very quick, keep it moving in the wok and don't over-cook.

RECIPE INDEX

First published in 2014 by New Holland Publishers Pty Ltd
London • Sydney • Auckland

The Chandlery Unit 114 50 Westminster Bridge Road London SE1 7QY United Kingdom
1/66 Gibbes Street Chatswood NSW 2067 Australia
218 Lake Road Northcote Auckland New Zealand

www.newhollandpublishers.com

Copyright © 2014 New Holland Publishers Pty Ltd
Copyright © 2014 in text: Jo Richardson
Copyright © 2014 in images: Joe Filshie except pp. 5,10 © Jack Sarafian; 14, 64, 135 © NHIL

All rights reserved. No part of this publication may be reproduced, stored in a retrieval system or transmitted, in any form or by any means, electronic, mechanical, photocopying, recording or otherwise, without the prior written permission of the publishers and copyright holders.

A record of this book is held at the British Library and the National Library of Australia.

ISBN 9781742575407

Managing director: Fiona Schultz
Publisher: Linda Williams
Project editor: Jodi De Vantier
Designer: Caryanne Cleevely
Photographs: Joe Filshie
Photography assistant: Geoff Magee
Food stylist: Georgie Dolling
Stylist's assistants: Katie Birchall, Regina Walter
Food for photography: Jo Richardson, Jo Forrest
Proofreader: Vicky Fisher
Production director: Olga Dementiev
Printer: Toppan Leefung Printing Ltd (China)
10 9 8 7 6 5 4 3 2 1

Our thanks to: Props co-op Sydney and Lilydale Chicken

Keep up with New Holland Publishers on Facebook
www.facebook.com/NewHollandPublishers